Second Wind

Second Wind

VARIATIONS ON A THEME OF GROWING OLDER

TOM PLUMMER

SHADOW
MOUNTAIN

Visit us at www.shadowmountain.com

Library of Congress Cataloging-in-Publication Data

Plummer, Tom.
   Second wind : variations on a theme of growing older / Tom Plummer.
     p.   cm.
   ISBN 1-57345-780-9
     1. Aging—United States—Psychological aspects.   I. Title.
   HQ1064.U5 P6   2000
   305.26'0973—dc21

                                        00-038748

Printed in the United States of America   72082-6672
10 9 8 7 6 5 4 3 2 1

For Al and Ginny Wirthlin

CONTENTS

INTRODUCTION:
AGING IN MY DIARY

By Louise Plummer

1982—Age 40: I am forty years old. I weigh 135 pounds and am 5 feet 9 1/2 inches tall. Every year I watch the Miss Universe contest. I am the right height for that contest. I watch it to see how close I am to the weight. The last time I was close to the weight was 1967. I am now ten pounds away from being Miss Universe. One of my front teeth is graying and a molar is chipped from eating a pretzel. It doesn't hurt, so I put off getting it fixed.

My husband, Tom, is a German professor at the University of Minnesota. I always thought I was like Jo March of *Little Women,* who wrote stories in her attic and married a German professor. I felt privileged, because there aren't enough German professors to go around for all the girls who read *Little Women* and thought themselves to be like Jo in every aspect. I find, now that I am forty, that not everyone wanted a German professor in the first place. I did, though.

1992—Age 50: It's 11:34 P.M. and I can't sleep, although I've tried; although my eyes itch; although I've taken one of those ten-hour antihistamines.

I look down and see my fat, loose stomach. I'm fifty and I've never been so fat. Fat and ugly. My son Sam won't let me put my bare foot on his lap because he is so repulsed by the corn on my foot. I can tell from my sons' faces that to their young eyes my body is hideous. Sam says my legs are like baloney with little spots of fat here and there.

I am discolored. Out in the sun too much. Splotchy everywhere.

Loose fat under my arms, on my thighs, and now this belly.

I smell bad, too. I am decaying at fifty. I never smelled bad when I was young. Now I have body odor. I'm physically disgusting. I have to paint myself up. I have to wear plenty of clothes. I have to have a perfect haircut. It's a lot of work now to look good. It's exhausting. I can see why some women give it up, but giving up makes you invisible. No one takes you seriously anymore.

Perhaps that would be a relief. Sexless, splotchy, crippled in one ankle, smelly, anxious, easily irritated. Who would notice such a woman? Who would love her?

Tom tells me a thousand time a day he loves me. He kisses me, tells me I'm beautiful, says what a wonderful woman I am. Says he is so lucky to have me—a hundred, a thousand times a day, he tells me; he shows me.

He weaves on the highway. "You're a terrible driver," I say.

"But you love me anyway," he says.

And I do.

1997—Age 55: I am fifty-five years old and thirty pounds overweight, but I don't have mood swings anymore—that alone might be worth the extra weight.

All my dreams have come true except I don't have a beach house, but I have friends who have beach houses and that is almost as good. I have gotten everything I've ever wanted, and everything from now on is sheer piggishness.

Lately I have started bathing with wind-up toys and rubber duckies. I have two rubber duckies, one that floats only on its side and one that floats upright. I have a porpoise, a whale, two tiny wooden boats, a penguin that paddles a rowboat, an alligator, a duck that flaps its wings, and a terry-cloth Ernie in a rubber tube. Some mornings it is hard to choose.

1999—Age 57: For my fifty-seventh birthday I made a trip to the hospital for an ultrasound test. The doctor wanted to have a close-up look at my useless ovaries. I lay on the table under a white sheet, my one fused foot sticking straight up in front of me.

When Sam was born twenty years ago, they either hadn't invented ultrasounds or didn't use them as readily as they do now, for example, to check out the sex of a new fetus. Dr. B. rubbed my stomach with lotion, then ran the hand-held camera across my abdomen. This was a check for cancer, not a peek at a fetus, so I avoided the monitor and stared up at the ceiling, trying not to feel like a carcass laid out as carrion.

"Ahh," the doctor sighed. I filled in the rest: "You're having a boy. A baby boy. Look, you can see him!" That was what I wanted my doctor to say, which goes to show that I don't get any wiser with age. I am fifty-seven and I want to have yet another newborn son. Foolish woman.

Instead, my doctor told me I didn't have cancer. Good news too, I know.

But if I *had* been pregnant at age fifty-seven, I would have driven straight from the hospital to Costco and bought a brand-new, white Jenny Lind crib that I could not afford twenty years ago and placed it in the upstairs bedroom next to ours. Then I would have found Tom and told him the good news.

PART 1

SIGNS AND SYMPTOMS

*"I fear I am not
in my perfect mind."*

—SHAKESPEARE, *KING LEAR*,
ACT IV, SCENE 7, LINE 50

Steady or Not, Here I Come

Several months ago when Louise and I were at the mall, I looked down and saw that I was wearing my house slippers. I recalled an uncle who always wore his house slippers when he came to visit, and I thought he was downright odd. My mother always said of such people, "He's kinda differ'nt, don'cha think?" And here I was staring at my feet and thinking of my uncle and hearing my mother say, "He's kinda differ'nt, don'cha think?"

I made the mistake of pointing out my gaffe to Louise. "Look," I said, "I'm wearing my house slippers." She broke into gales of laughter. She stood in the open mall, her hand on her forehead, her mouth wide open, hee-hawing.

"What's so funny about that?" I wanted to know.

This brought even harder laughing. "You're turning into an old man," she said. "I can't wait to tell our friends that you've started wearing your house slippers to the mall."

Not long afterward, when Louise was in New York and I was no longer under her watchful eye, our friends Al and Ginny invited me to go to dinner. It might have been a this-guy-is-alone-and-needs-some-company-before-he-goes-nuts consolation prize. Friends have observed that I become loony when left alone for more than twenty-four hours; they try to watch out for me. I readily accepted their invitation and arrived at their house at the appointed hour. I had no sooner entered their front hall than I looked down and saw that I was again wearing my house slippers.

"I've forgotten something," I said. "I'll be right back." I jumped in the car, raced home, put on real shoes, and sped back to Al and Ginny's.

"Ready," I said. "Let's go."

"What was that all about?" Al wanted to know.

"I was wearing my house slippers," I said. "I had to put on street shoes."

"We wouldn't care if you wore your house slippers to a restaurant," Ginny said.

"You don't understand," I said. "I really have to wear shoes. If Louise ever found out I'd worn my house slippers to a restaurant, I'd never hear the end of it."

When Louise came home from New York, we again went out to eat with Al and Ginny.

"Did you know," Al said to Louise over bisque at the Capitol Cafe, "that Tom wore his house slippers to dinner the other night?"

I suppose wearing house slippers in public is a sign of absentmindedness in aging. It may even signify that I'm just a bit "differ'nt." But "differ'nt" from what? I certainly hope "differ'nt" from the teenagers I see around town. When I went to high school, the "preppy" look was in. For guys that meant neatly pressed khaki slacks, a cotton, button-down shirt, and matching shoes—penny loafers or tan oxfords from Florsheim's. That wasn't "differ'nt." That was classic.

"Differ'nt," in my late-middle-aged view, is Dr. Martens shoes, which are the rage among younger people. For those lucky enough to have finished raising their children more than ten years ago, let me explain that Dr. Martens are among the ugliest footwear ever to hit the planet. Their hallmark, in a word, is bulk. Morbid obesity. They are so robust that the manufacturer claims in one promo, "While in Bosnia, BBC correspondent Kate Adie came under attack, and two pieces of shrapnel pierced her foot. She says that her Dr. Martens boots saved her foot by absorbing most of the shock from the blast." But to say that the single quality of this footwear is mass is to oversimplify the matter and widens the chasm between me and the younger generation. In an attempt to narrow the gap, I have searched and learned more from the Dr. Martens Web site, **www.drmartens.com**. What I discovered is the following:

Dr. Martens shoes come in a variety of styles: Classics, Street, Urban, Open AirWair, Terrain, Steel (meaning steel-toed boots and shoes), and Catwalk (a line for women). There are photographs of shoes and boots, if they can be called that, in each category. I am particularly intrigued with the "Steel" group because, when I was a much younger man, guys who wore steel-toed boots were either construction-type workers needing extra foot protection or proto-Nazis who wanted to break someone else's shins.

Besides the general categories, which appeal to a wide range of needs for young people, three things seem to be of crucial importance: the stitching, the soles, and the colors. Each calls for some attention. In examining my son's Dr. Martens, I noticed—I had not noticed before because I am aesthetically challenged—that the stitching is coarse and prominent. The most common stitching is yellow, with one-half inch spacing between the holes (I have measured this to be as precise as possible), referred to as a "Yellow Z Stitch." This, of course, calls attention to itself because the soles appear to have been attached to the upper shoe with a low-quality, non-floating fishing line. The Web site also mentions other stitching: Self Stitch (does that mean you do it yourself?), and, in women's shoes, Burgundy Abilene and Black Abilene. Who or what Abilene is remains a mystery to me, although a song comes to mind: "O Abilene, Sweet Abilene."

In the more conservative models for guys, the soles are about one inch thick, and the heels add another three-quarters of an inch. In extreme cases, soles may be two or three times that thick. The soles add considerable weight to the shoes. When I stood on the bathroom scale and held my son's shoes, they added five pounds to my weight. Walking around the block in those shoes would be the equivalent of a three-mile run for me. If I wore them to the mall, I'd have to stagger back to my car within minutes after I left it. I can walk all day in my house slippers.

But thickness is only one aspect of the soles. The other is the variety of cleated bottoms, which come with their own labels. BEN is widely used for both boots and shoes. Sam's, I believe, are BEN soles. They appear to be of some kind of hardened, rubbery substance, and on the bottom is imprinted:

OIL
FAT
ACID
PETROL
ALKALI
RESISTANT

These words are listed vertically, without punctuation, so it is not clear to me if oil, fat, acid, petrol, and alkali are part of the makeup of the sole, which is a worrisome thought, or whether the sole is impervious to these substances, which would come as no surprise. Other styles include DMS, BEX, ENVY, and BUZZ.

That the soles are an important component of the shoes' appeal is attested to by the fact that Web-site visitors can click on the picture of a given shoe and get a close-up of the bottom of the sole, revealing the tread. This is where I realized that the BEX soles sported by some of the "Street" shoes have about as much tread on them as my Jeep Grand Cherokee's tires, and that the ENVY soles appear to have bear claws affixed to the bottom, even though they, too, are supposed to be suitable for street wear, perhaps for clawing urban attackers to death.

I find that I'm most attracted to the Dr. Martens colors, advertised as Black Greasy, Aztec Crazy Horse, Black Smooth, White Smooth, Navy Smooth, Cherry Red Smooth, Black Grizzly, Peanut Grizzly, Bark Grizzly, Black Fine Haircell, and, my personal favorite, Cherry Red Fine Haircell, which I discovered on an excursion with my son Sam one day to Nordstrom's, where some Dr. Martens boots were on sale. These were calf-high men's boots, a choice of bright red or yellow, with gold glitter. I picked up the red one and held it out for Sam to see. It glistened like the sun turned to blood. Sam was standing at a rack of shoes several feet away. "Hey, Sam," I said in a loud voice, "I'm thinking about buying these to wear to class. How do you think my students would react?"

His face went scarlet. He looked to see if anyone was around and said, "Shhhh."

"What do you mean, 'Shhhh?'" I said. I raised my voice a decibel or two. "I like these Dr. Martens. They're cool."

Realizing I could not be controlled, he walked away.

So Dr. Martens are for young folks, and house slippers are for old guys. I rather like wearing my house slippers. They have thin, inconspicuous soles, suede tops with, I admit, a large stitch down the middle on top, and comfortable, fake-sheepskin lining. They don't cry out for attention, they keep my feet warm, and I can walk for long distances without becoming dehydrated. Best of all, they're absolutely nonviolent: I couldn't kick anyone's shins without hurting myself.

Louise says that I've got it wrong, that Dr. Martens are for young folks and house slippers are for old geezers who can't remember to put on their shoes. Wearing house slippers in public is a sign of instability. Her thinking comes close to that of Jean Paul when he wrote, "The young man is deliberately odd and prides himself on it, the old man is unintentionally so, and it mortifies him."

Close, but no truffle. My house slippers do not mortify me. They mortify Louise. I find Goethe's thinking more in line with my feelings on the subject: "It does not become a man of years to follow the fashion, either in his thinking or his dress." Goethe was a classy guy. I'll take his word for it. I'm not going to follow the fashion of the young folks, that's for sure. As for my thinking, maybe I am a little wobbly in the head, but steady or not, here I come.

You Know You're Getting Older When . . .

A list compiled by Tom and Louise and Al and Ginny over light supper at the Urban Bistro.

You know you're getting older when . . .

• your feet hurt in the morning, and you haven't gone anywhere yet.

• people mistake you for your father's brother.

• you mention phonograph records and the young people in the room don't know what you're talking about.

• you can't read the numbers on the remote control, but it doesn't matter because everything on television seems so stupid.

- young people refer to folks your age as "really old."
- you start watching where you lay things in your bedroom at night so you don't trip on them when you make nocturnal trips to the bathroom.
- your main source of entertainment is the televised infomercials at 2:00 in the morning.
- you actually buy infomercial products.
- you start looking for shoes that fit comfortably and look lousy rather than shoes that look great and feel lousy.
- you read the obituaries before anything else in the newspaper.
- you start saying things like, "We can't take that trip. We have to save our money."
- your crystal goblets have gotten dusty.
- you can't remember the names of friends and neighbors from the distant past and call them "yuh," as in, "Oh, my gosh, how are yuh? It's so good to see yuh. Haven't seen yuh in ages. How're all yer kids?"
- your doctor says, "Learn to live with it."

SLEEPLESS
IN HAWAII

If you have a solution for getting a good night's sleep—a deep sleep, where you wake up in the morning feeling like the folks in those ads on TV who smile and stretch as they sit up on their body-contour mattresses and say, "That was just divine"—I'd like to hear from you. And I don't mean that I want to get letters from people praising melatonin or Sominex. I'm looking for a real solution here. Where are the experts when you need them?

Sleep has become a problem. I can't even get a good night's sleep on vacation in Hawaii. One day a note appeared on the door of the condo where we were staying:

——ATTENTION——
YOUR UNIT WILL BE SPRAYED WITH
PESTICIDES ON TUESDAY, JAN. 19, AT 9:00 A.M.
    IF YOU SUFFER FROM ANY RESPIRATORY AIL-
MENT OR ARE ALLERGIC TO ANY CHEMICALS,
PLEASE VACATE THE PREMISES FOR 3 HOURS.
    SORRY FOR THE INCONVENIENCE
    329–4518
    BIG ISLAND PEST CONTROL, INC.
    BETTER HEALTH THRU PEST CONTROL

Apart from the double-speak of this notice—better
health through a poison environment—a note like this
poses a problem. We aren't out of the house by
9:00 A.M. on vacation. We might not be out of the
house by 11:00 A.M. except to run to the store for
macadamia-nut Danishes that we can eat in bed. On the
other hand, both of us have some respiratory problems,
and the notion of clinging to our late-morning habits at
the risk of being fumigated does not appeal.

"We'll just lay out our clothes and leave early,"
Louise said. "We can go to Kona and then on to the vol-
cano tomorrow."

This made sense that evening. But I began waking
several hours early to see if it was time to get up. Yes, I
set the clock-radio alarm, but it was not a familiar appa-
ratus to me, so I wasn't sure it would work. I dozed off
until 2:30 and woke up every half hour thereafter.

I suppose I fell into a deeper sleep at about 6:00 A.M., because when the alarm went off, not with the music station I had selected but with a loud buzzing noise that sounded like an incoming F-16, I jolted out of bed. With a headache.

I'd really like to blame the pesticide guys for that lousy night's sleep, but even on quiet nights when I don't have to clear the premises for fumigators, I'm often awake by 4:00 A.M. From what I hear, it's a problem for many people who have passed the fifty-year marker.

As a teenager who could sleep for ten or twelve hours without half trying, I used to listen unsympathetically to my octogenarian grandmother saying that she never slept past four in the morning. At the magic hour, sleep became tossing and turning, thrashing around until 6:30 or so, when it was time to get up, she said. She would heave a big sigh as if mourning a great loss. Now that I'm in the same boat, I not only understand the problem, I regret not being more sympathetic with my grandmother.

Louise, on the other hand, has a different twist on the problem. If she goes to bed before 1:00 in the morning, she can't go to sleep. What's more, her best inducement to sleep is television, which she watches in our bedroom. This has been the source of some adjustments in our relationship. Not wanting to switch to two bedrooms, I have learned to go to sleep around 10:30 in the middle of *Law and Order* reruns, wake up around 1:30 when Louise is asleep, turn off the TV—it's a good night when I can find the remote control—and fall asleep again until 4:00, when I'm wide awake and she's out cold.

I have slowly given in to the idea that it is better to get up on these early mornings than to lie in bed and think about doing something. Usually this means putting on a robe and slippers, going downstairs to the living room, and, unless it is insufferably hot, lighting a fire. The fire seems to disentangle my snarled mind. My nervous system quits jumping around like a flea circus, and I try to listen to my breathing and think of nothing at all. The harder it is to think of nothing, to keep my mind from racing, the more I realize I am out of control.

Although this sleeplessness gives me the sense that I am the only human being on the planet awake in the night, a quick search on the Internet for *insomnia* assures me I am not. There I find dozens of listings, including an abstract from a medical journal, *Archives of Internal Medicine,* reporting the unsavory information that "patients with chronic insomnia are more likely to develop affective disorders, cardiac morbidity, and other adverse health outcomes."

Then comes the advice from a physician: "Patients

should be educated about the importance of 'good sleep hygiene,' such as setting a regular time to go to bed and avoiding daytime naps." Thank you very much.

Another Web site contains a report by the U.S. Public Health Service that classifies insomnia as either transient, intermittent, or chronic. This is an old academic trick. If you can't solve a problem, break it into parts and classify them. There are two kinds of snakes in the world: poisonous and nonpoisonous.

Chronic insomnia is the most troublesome, the report continues, because there may be underlying causes: depression, asthma, and restless-legs syndrome. I don't know what restless-legs syndrome is, but it sounds utterly intriguing. I could add a short in the electric blanket to that list. Shorts were a serious problem in my family. My dad's cousin, Theo Anderson, loved to apply his training as an electrical engineer to lacing a mattress with wiring that he attached to a transformer. When someone retired to the bed and dozed off, Theo would turn on the juice, resulting in a lot of hollering. Then, still not knowing what had awakened him, the victim would return to bed, fall asleep, and begin the cycle again. This roundelay would continue until the insomniac finally got smart and ripped off the sheets to discover that his bed had been wired. Hence I include wired-bed syndrome among the causes of chronic insomnia.

Now thoroughly bored and anesthetized by the clinical language of the U.S. Public Health Service, I find an Internet chat room called "Pillow Talk," where people write in to talk with other insomniacs about their problems and to hear suggestions or at least get sympathy. This is where all the medical jargon, the cold, distant language like "sociodemographics," "insomnia-comorbidity," and "subthreshhold depression," hits the fan. This is where people's guts go online. The first letter is from Isabelle, who has twice failed her bar exams to become a certified lawyer. (It seems to me that she lucked out and should look for a productive career, but that's just my opinion.) Before going to bed, she has tried drinking warm milk, sipping red wine, making the room too hot, making the room too cold, listening to music, having someone play guitar and lullabies (I don't know how I'd go to sleep with someone doing that in my bedroom), and taking herbal pills (I understand charcoal and birch bark pills are really effective, but if you overdose, watch out for woodpeckers).

So she knows she's going to have trouble with insomnia and fail the exam for the third time unless she gets some sleep. What should she do? she asks.

I sympathize completely with Isabelle. I went through a doctoral program. Doctoral programs, like other professional programs, don't let you finish without administering several hazings. In a doctoral program, the first of these hazings after the coursework is completed is called the "general examination." For me this consisted of having a body of literature about the size of Mother Russia—240 novels and plays and all the major poetry written in the German language from the ninth to the twentieth centuries—in my head, complete with commentaries, at least to the point that I could engage in some intelligible discussion of any given work.

About a month before my general examination, I began to suffer from serious sleep deprivation. Two weeks before the exam, I wasn't sleeping at all, just lying in bed quivering and staring at the ceiling. The exam was scheduled for the first week in January, and I knew for sure that I'd meet with the same fate Isabelle describes if I didn't finally get some Zs.

On New Year's Eve I told Louise I couldn't engage in any festivities. I had to go to bed. A friend gave me some heavy-duty sleep medication. I went to bed at 10:00 P.M. and, lo, fell asleep. I was awakened by the telephone at midnight. It was Lorin Pugh. I am using his real name here because I don't think the guilty should ever be protected. Lorin knew my plight, knew I was staying away from a party, knew I had gone to bed. This was fodder for Lorin's cannon.

"Hi, Tom," he said in a cheery voice laced with snickering. "Happy New Year."

I yelled. I yelled loud. Something helpless like, "Lorin, you dirty rat."

He laughed and laughed. He thought he was so darn funny. "I just wanted to wish you happy New Year," he said.

I raged into the bedroom yelling. "That rotten Lorin. He knew why I went to bed early."

Unlike Isabelle, I did pass the exam, and I still consider Lorin my friend, but I'll never forgive him.

Another chat room person is a woman who's married to an insomniac. He tosses and turns while he's trying to get to sleep; she feels rejected because she can't fall asleep in his arms; she hangs on to her side of the bed so she won't disturb him. How can she help him? she wonders.

Many of the writers say they are anxious and afraid—anxious that they won't go to sleep and afraid that they'll die if they don't. This results in the day-to-day "zombie syndrome."

Then there's the hooked-on-prescription-drugs group. One fellow writes that he was able to quit them, "but only after the most painful ordeal of my life—I couldn't sleep at all for three days and felt terrified, deeply depressed." Others say cutting out drugs "cold turkey" is "hell," "dangerous," and "anxiety producing."

So what's the answer? Who knows? All this talk about insomnia leaves me convinced that no one has an answer. You can ignore insomnia and hope it goes away. You can take drugs and hope you don't get addicted. You can lie awake all night or you can get up and do something. There's always infomercials. It all makes me very anxious. And sleepy. Very sleepy.

I think I'm going to lie down for a nap while I can get one.

PART 2

SEPARATION AND REUNION

"What scares me the most is that my kids will stop taking me seriously and start treating me like I don't know anything."

—FRIEND, IN HER SIXTIES

"When you talk, I get the hiccups."

—ANNE, AGE FIVE,
TALKING TO HER MOTHER, AGE TWENTY-TWO

You Aren't Supposed to Smell the Same

I turned thirty in 1969. That was a bad year to turn thirty, because it was the peak of America's youthful revolution against the "establishment," which meant anyone thirty or older was the enemy, out of date, stale. I witnessed the upheaval. One late morning in 1966, I picked up Louise from her job in University Hall, one of the administrative nerve centers of Harvard, and took her to lunch at Brigham's. We probably had corn chowder and a slice of French bread, a dietary pleasure that I had learned from Louise. If things went as they always did, Louise ate her chowder of cream, corn, and bits of bacon while popping her lips and saying, "Mmmmmm. I just love this."

I loved her passion even more than the chowder. After strolling around Harvard Square for a bit, probably browsing in a bookstore or two and walking through Design Research, a modernist store for the up-and-coming generation, we returned to campus.

There we discovered that, while we had been eating lunch, the entire world had changed. A crowd of students and faculty stood outside University Hall, looking up at precisely the windows to the room where Louise worked. A revolutionary group on campus had occupied the building, told the administrators to leave, and proceeded to rifle through the files or just sit in the second-floor windows and let their feet dangle out. The mood at the time was still jocular, the students in the windows cracking jokes with their classmates below while the faculty looked on bemused, possibly thinking this was a passing fancy.

It was not a passing fancy, and when fears arose later that evening that files and documents would be destroyed, the police moved in. News reports showed the Cambridge cops bashing the brains out of some of America's brightest students. The mood on campus turned somber, even funereal, as we all realized that an age of bliss and naiveté had died quite suddenly after a

brief struggle with a nervous condition fueled by the
Vietnam War.

Out of this national confusion of the 1960s arose
the unfortunate notion that anyone my age or older
could not possibly understand what was going on in
the minds of younger people. This was accentuated by
a number of icons that distinguished the new from the
old. Like clothing. When I began graduate school in
1965, it was simply understood that the men wore suits
and ties to class and the women dresses or skirts and
blouses with jackets. If a guy felt extremely casual, he
might wear a sports jacket and tie. Harvard's dining
rooms required that every male student wear a jacket
and tie for meals. After the beginning of the revolution,
men began appearing at lunch with jackets and ties but
wearing T-shirts.

The term *generation gap* emerged sometime in that
period. Generation gaps have always existed in the
form of power struggles between older and younger
people, a fact that ancient Greek writers have verified
in their condemnations of young people. But I don't
think the line between the young and the not-so-young,
meaning people over thirty, had ever been drawn quite
so clearly. If you were over thirty, you became part of
the "establishment" and, in the minds of the younger
generation, part of the problem. So on October 21,
1969, I joined the "establishment," not by choice but

by definition. I didn't like it, but there I was. And there I have remained.

I suppose I could say, therefore, that my official entry into aging began when I turned thirty. It was a sociological definition imposed by the times. Over the years, my sons have reinforced this notion in more ways than I could have possibly imagined.

No one convinces me so pointedly that the law of the jungle applies to me as my sons. The young guys beat up the old guys, whether we're talking about Bambi driving off his dad or the good old human practice of getting down in the dirt with the boys and showing them who's boss—until one fine day they show the old guy who is boss. Survival of the fittest, Darwin called it. The older I get, the less fit I am.

The task for me has shifted from the physical to the mental, and the question to be solved, again and again, is, how do I outwit them and thus keep them at bay? In this light, the bleak future becomes a whole lot brighter because, as they say in the old German movies, "I schtill haff my vays."

The trick, I'm learning, is to be ever on the lookout for their subtle assaults on my dignity. One evening, for example, I was sitting with Louise and Sam, our seventeen-year-old son, in the living room, just hanging out. The mood was peaceful. We were a model family, a nuclear family. I felt safe.

Sam said he needed deodorant.

"We do too," I said.

"Yeah," Louise said. "You could pick up some deodorant for us."

"I'm not going to the same store you go to," he said.

"What store did you think we were going to?" I asked.

"Well, what I mean is, they only have my kind of deodorant at Dan's and Payless," he said.

"That's okay," I said. "Just get us the kind you get, that stuff with the gray cap. That's good stuff."

"No way," he said. "I don't want you guys wearing the same deodorant I wear."

"What do you mean?" Louise and I said in unison. I pointed out, "You have your deodorant in one bathroom, and we have ours in another." We thought he meant he was worried that we might use his deodorant and get our aging, underarm cooties on his deodorant stick and cause some kind of grotesque malformations to occur in his body, like sagging arms and a pot belly.

That was not what he meant. "You can't wear the same deodorant as your parents. You aren't supposed to smell the same as your parents."

"What are you talking about?" I asked. "The only way you can smell someone else's deodorant is by sticking your nose in their armpits. They only do that in deodorant ads."

"Well, can't I just get you guys the deodorant with the green cap?" He was starting to whine. "You like that too, don't you?"

To tell the truth, I couldn't tell the difference. I was tempted to inflame the hostilities but bit my tongue. "Yeah, that's okay too," I said. "But," and I pulled out my one remaining weapon, "I'm going to put this conversation in a book."

"You'd better watch out what you say around here," Louise said. "You'll find yourself in print."

CHINESE CHECKERS TORTURE

My Grandmother Swindle knew about power and children. Whenever she had a chance, she would whomp me. Now I can almost hear her protesting, "I never whomped you. I loved you."

Yes, Grandma, you loved me, but you also whomped me. Your theory of child rearing, I see with hindsight, was "To love them is to whomp them."

When my parents went out for the evening, Grandma, who lived with us, followed a routine. She washed and I dried the dishes; she cleaned off countertops, swept the floor, and took off her apron. Taking off the apron was her battle cry. It was like guys in a bar taking off their jackets for a fight. She would say, "Do you want to play a game?" I had no preferable alternative. In my preadolescent years, evening television for boys wasn't up to much. My favorite show was the *Buck Rogers* serial, and that was over by 7:00.

She had no alternative either. Her favorites came on Sunday nights: *What's My Line* and *The Red Skelton Show.* She loved the original *What's My Line* people— Dorothy Kilgallen, Arlene Frances, Fred Allen, Bennett Cerf, and John Daly—loved to watch them try to guess the bizarre occupations of the guests before the winnings went up to fifty dollars. And I suspect she adored the classy panel for their New York accents, their gentle humor, and their keen wit.

Red Skelton, by contrast, was a clown. His batty eyes, crumpled hat, and slurred speech were stock parts of *The Red Skelton Show.* He'd tell a joke and then laugh at it. He'd act like he was trying to stifle his laughing but couldn't, and his whole body would shake. "Oh, dear, he's funny," Grandma would say, her body quivering in unison with his.

What Red Skelton shared with the *What's My Line* folks, I now realize, was a philosophy about humor. "If some day you're not feeling well," Skelton said once, "you should remember some little thing I have said or done, and if it brings a smile to your face or a chuckle to your heart, then my purpose as a clown has been fulfilled."

"A clown is a warrior who fights gloom," he said on another occasion. At the root of his humor was an idea about the absurdity of human nature: "A comedian is the most serious man in the world," he said, "because he must know his fellow man so well that he can mime and imitate him without hating him completely."

So if it was too late for *Buck Rogers* and the wrong day for comedy, it was game time. Game time did not mean friendly time. It did not mean a nice little old lady being sweet to her grandson. Game time for Grandma meant beating me and laughing about it. It meant food-chain time.

Grandma would go to her chest of drawers and retrieve the marbles that she must have had for sixty or seventy years. She stored them in a box that had once contained Russell Stover's chocolates. Now it was tattered, its once white cover grayed with age. Some of the marbles were missing, so only the blacks and whites were a complete set. Typically she took white and I took black.

"Go get the card table," she would say. She did not mean just any card table, certainly not one of the newer Samsonite tables that my parents had purchased. She meant her special card table, which she had brought with her many years before from Monroe, Utah, a fancy one with wooden legs and a geometric design in the middle.

I would retrieve the ritual table and set it up in the living room. She would ceremoniously set out the

marbles and her Chinese checkers board, which must
have been as old as the marbles. It was framed with
black metal, and its worn surface attested to hundreds
if not thousands of games.

"Do you want to start?" she would ask. Usually I let
her begin. I wanted to study her moves. Grandma had a
standard set of openings. I could imitate them up to a
point and then my game fell apart. Without ever knowing quite how she did it, I found her blocking my
moves while advancing her marbles, hooting and cack-
ling. She gave all the more impression of launching a
carefully conceived carnage because she was so delib-
erate in her moves. With her shaky hands she would
pick up a marble slowly, and then touch it down in
each hole as she moved it across the board, like a very
old rabbit jumping hop by hop across a field. I found
this irritating; I liked to see just where the marble was
going to be and set it down there without making the
intermediate jumps. Grandma challenged my impetu-
ous moves from time to time, requiring that I show her
exactly how I got from A to B.

Sometimes with her palsy she would drop a marble
or jar the whole board, causing all the marbles to roll
around. Then we'd have to reconstruct the game. It
seemed to me at such moments that I should be able to
beat this clumsy old woman.

It was a delusion of youth. When the game was

over, and I sat despairing that Grandma had beaten me yet again, she'd laugh and laugh, take off her glasses, wipe her eyes, adjust her dentures, and say, "Oh, dear, kids are funny. Would you like to play again?"

After my mother died, my sister and I set about cleaning out her house. In a closet I found my grandmother's Chinese checkers board. In a drawer I found the marbles, still in the Russell Stover's candy box. In the basement I found the card table. "I want these," I said to my sister. I took them home. And although I haven't figured out what to do with them, just seeing them makes me happy. I can't use the game, because no one will play me. I whomp 'em every time.

TALES OF THE ROAD

When I was twenty-two, I traveled through Europe with my parents and was often embarrassed by my father's impatience with European ways. It didn't occur to me then that letting his opinions be known in such vocal fashion may have been due in part to his age. He just wasn't going to put up anymore with things he didn't like.

When my parents arrived in Vienna, I had already been there for thirty months. I felt half Austrian. I wanted to immerse them in Austrian ways as I had been immersed. A friend in his fifties, however, advised that I give them a chance to undergo culture shock in a more comfortable way. Neither had ever been abroad, he reminded me.

"Your parents aren't twenty-two," he said. "They'll want some time to get adjusted."

I picked them up at the airport and booked them in

the Regina, a three-star hotel just off the Ring sur-
rounding the inner city, steps from the Rathaus and the
Votivkirche.

My senior adviser had suggested it. This would be
just what they needed. Dad, after all, was sixty-three,
Mother fifty-nine. My father wasn't in top shape; my
mother had spent the entire spring undergoing painful
dental surgery; her mother had died just five months
before. Yes, they could use a nice hotel and a decent
bed. They needed to recover.

They felt differently. Yes, they needed to recover, but
not in an expensive room that cost ten dollars a night
in 1962. They didn't need a hotel that nice, they said,
they could have done just fine with a cheaper place. I
held my ground, pointing out that they could see
almost everything of interest by taking short walks
from the hotel. They ended up staying in the Regina,
somewhat assuaged when I told them European breakfast was included in the price of the room.

The next day I met them for breakfast at the hotel's
outdoor restaurant, tables decked with white linen
cloths and napkins, crystal goblets and china. My
mother was charmed. She loved a well-set table.
Breakfast for her would be fine because the setting was
beautiful. My father, still a bit grumpy about the cost of
the room, was waiting to see if breakfast would be
worth it. Would it be the breakfast my mother fixed

him every day of their married life: bacon, eggs, toast, oatmeal, juice, and coffee?

The waiter brought breakfast on a silver tray and set it ceremoniously in front of them—Austrian *Semmeln* or hard rolls, strawberry jam, and butter. Would they care for coffee, tea, or juice? the waiter asked. My dad stared at the basket of rolls in disbelief.

"That's breakfast?" he said. "That's not breakfast. I want an egg and some bacon."

"I'm zorry, zir," the waiter replied in his broken English, "vee don't haff tsat on arr menyew."

Breakfasts of eggs and bacon were just not available even in three-star hotels in postwar Austria. Bread and butter and jam were what the Austrians were eating, and that was what Dad was going to eat. He complained again to the waiter, who just shrugged his shoulders.

"Relax, Dad," I said. "That's what they eat."

"That's not breakfast," he repeated.

The rolls had a hard crust. Dad said something about baseballs when he took his first bite. My mother was having a hard time too; her gums were still sore from the surgery. She soaked the *Semmeln* in her drink to soften them.

To my young chagrin, when the waiter returned to the table, Dad told him what he thought of the lousy breakfast. Again the waiter shrugged him off.

"I need an egg for breakfast," Dad muttered as he and Mom went back to their room.

This episode was symptomatic of what was to come when we arrived in Florence two weeks later after having visited Salzburg, the Austrian Alps, and Venice. Several days on the road in a Volkswagen Beetle had convinced even Dad that he needed a comfortable night. "We'll get a nice room with hot water," he said to Mom, who was as anxious as he was to find a few of the pleasures of home.

Searching through the tourist guides, we found a hotel in the heart of the city. "Does the room have running water?" my dad asked the desk clerk.

"Yes, sir," the clerk answered.

Dad signed on.

Once in the room, he started the bath water. He wanted a good soak. The water ran and ran and ran, becoming colder and colder.

"There's no hot water," he said. He uttered a few curses from his repertoire. "I'm going down to complain."

I went along. I had heard my dad voice his opinions before, had read his letters recounting fights with the mayor and state legislature over funding for a new public library in Salt Lake City, but nothing I had heard compared with his form that day in front of the Florentine desk clerk.

"We paid for a room with running water," he said. "I asked you if there was running water in the room and you said there was. There is no hot water to take a bath. What kind of *&%*@^# were you giving me?"

I hoped the clerk could get only the drift of his words and not their precise meaning.

"Yes, there is running water in the room," the clerk said in a stiff European manner.

"There's no hot water," Dad yelled. "I paid for a room with hot water."

"You paid for a room with running water," the desk clerk said. "The hotel has no hot water today." He held both arms out, palms up, and shrugged.

Dad sputtered, protested, but in the end lost.

I was embarrassed. My father was a man of distinction, a man of fine reputation. He had gone over the top with this protest, I thought.

I think differently now. After years of locking horns with university administrations, city engineers, and, yes, hotel desk clerks, I'm ready to do a bit of yelling myself. What's there to lose? At worst, someone can shrug me off as a crazy old man. Louise has learned to put up with this side of me—up to a point. When I get my feathers ruffled, she calls me the little banty rooster.

It was in that frame of mind that I wrote the following letter to the Keltic Lodge in Nova Scotia:

June 21, 1999
TO: Management,
Keltic Lodge,
Cape Breton, Nova Scotia
FROM: Thomas G. Plummer

This is a multifaceted complaint about the services of the world-famous, multiple-starred Keltic Lodge of Cape Breton, the one that advertises on page 184 of the Nova Scotia 1999 Complete Guide for Doers & Dreamers: "Come nightfall, experience the hospitality, gourmet cuisine and Island entertainment for which Keltic Lodge is renowned."

On Wednesday, June 16, 1999, my wife, Louise, and I headed out from Caribou River with our friends Norma and Garold Davis and our little white dog, Zoe. This would be the ride to end all rides. Seascapes, mountainscapes, rolling countryside with farmlands nestled into forests, ending at the Keltic Lodge. We drove along the Sunrise Trail past Antigonish to Port Hastings, where we stopped for tourist information and souvenirs. From Port Hastings I called the Keltic Lodge to inquire about rooms for that evening. Two rooms were indeed available, the courteous reservations clerk informed me, at the rate of $268 per night. While I was catching my breath at this price quotation, she hastened to add that the room price included the Lodge's legendary four-course evening meal and breakfast. Dinner was available until 9:00 P.M., she *assured me, in case we arrived late. Moderate-modest-decent (the exact adjective escapes me) dress was required for the evening meal, she added.*

Being a bit of a prude myself, I assumed this meant shirts, shoes, socks, and the like. Clean, tasteful, jeans would surely be acceptable at a golf resort. I announced to my fellow travelers that we were putting out a bundle of cash, but that this would be well worth it. We would have lovely rooms in a spectacular setting and unrivaled cuisine.

We made our way northeastward through Port Hood, Inverness, Cap Le Moine, Cheticamp, and Cape North. When driving became a bit tiresome, we reminded ourselves that we were going to a wonderful resort with world-famous food. The anticipation sustained us through the long drive. At 6:00 P.M. we arrived at Ingonish and the Keltic Lodge. We ooohed and aaahed at the dramatic ocean scenery, the tree-lined and flowered drive up to the lodge, and the interior of the lodge itself. At the desk we learned we would not be staying in the lodge per se but in a new facility just across from the Atlantic Restaurant. That would be fine. The rooms were larger, we learned. The desk clerk also told us to make reservations for dinner in the main lodge before going to our rooms. It was now about 6:10 P.M.

Garold and I salivated toward the dining room, where a courteous and efficient hostess informed us that, since other groups had booked the dining room for most of the evening, we could eat only at 6:50. Acceptable dress excluded denims, she added. I was wearing khakis, but others in the group had denims. Was my denim shirt worthy for the royal ambiance? What did denim *include?*

My wife and I took room 502, the Davises room 600. Once in the room, I informed my wife about the "d"-word. "That's all I have," she said. "I don't have anything else to wear." I was willing to have a confrontation at the restaurant, hollering my head off in front of appalled patrons about the lack of information and demanding admission. My wife—you may thank your lucky stars—was not.

In the meantime, we had become aware of the sorely inadequate soundproofing between us and the adjacent room, where we could hear conversation with no trouble at all. Then we noticed that elephants were housed overhead. We heard their every step as they lumbered from one side of the room to the other. The room's insulation was about as good as that of the army barracks I lived in forty years ago.

I decided to appeal the dress standards by telephone. I reached a polite male voice in the dining room who said there was no way we could eat there. "Then where do you want us to eat?" I demanded.

He said we could eat in the Atlantic, just across the road from where we were staying. "You will have a wonderful meal there," he said. I felt reassured. I was a sucker.

At the Atlantic, Davises ordered salmon; we ordered steak. The salmon was dry; the steak was tough and over-cooked. Dessert might bring some relief, we thought. I tried the blueberry pie, which had almost no flavor in the berries, which were packed between two slabs of raw pie dough.

The Davises decided to go for a walk, at least to catch a bit of the nature scenery around the lodge. We went back to the hotel room, where my wife decided to do what she always does after an irritating experience: take a hot bath. She ran the bath for several minutes and got nothing but barely lukewarm water.

By now I had had enough. We were paying $268 for a cheaply built room with no hot water and a lousy meal. We would have done far better at a Motel 6 and a decent restaurant. I stormed up to the front desk and encountered a very efficient night manager, who apologized for the inconvenience and irritation, agreed that I was justifiably angry, and promised to have the maintenance people fix the hot water. By the time I got back to the room, she had called and informed my wife that our room rate would be adjusted by $45. I could only scoff. That brought the basic rate down to $223, which, given the circumstances, was outrageous. My wife convinced me to back off and go to bed, which I did, only to be awakened in the night by heavy feet tromping overhead and shrill voices penetrating the steel door separating us from the people in the *adjoining room. It was 2:00 A.M. I went to the bathroom and checked for hot water. There was none.*

The next morning, we went to the main lodge to see if we could get breakfast in our denims. We were admitted. It was raining outside, and I had in hand my favorite umbrella, purchased at Bloomingdales in New York. A young man suggested I put it in a rack with a bunch of other umbrellas that looked a lot like it. Although I had some hesitation about this, I didn't want to risk being deprived of breakfast. I deposited the umbrella in the rack, along with a smaller umbrella we were carrying tucked inside so that neither would be mistaken by someone else.

Breakfast was good. Not as good as we had eaten at the Dalvay House on Prince Edward Island, but it was good. We left to pack and check out, only to discover my umbrella had been stolen. It was the last straw. The staff wandered around bleating, wondering what to do about the umbrella, wringing their hands, and shrugging their shoulders. Finally I left my mailing address, signed my bill under protest, and left. On the way out I cursed the Keltic Lodge and promised never to return. Furthermore, I will tell everyone I know to be sure to see Cape Breton but avoid the Keltic Lodge.

Sincerely,
Tom Plummer

I showed Louise the letter. "Don't bother sending it," she said. "They won't do anything about it. Your letter is overkill. You could just tell them the accommodations were unsatisfactory."

I didn't send it. I'm just sharing it wherever possible. It's one of the lovely things about aging—you can say what you want when you want. There's no more social climbing to be concerned with, no more greasing of hands. No fear. Let it all hang out.

My friend Garold Davis feels differently. Be nice, that's his policy. He did not complain at the desk about his cold water.

I told him that I had complained and that they had reduced my room price by $45. When we went together to check out, the desk clerk presented the bills to us side by side.

Garold's bill was $268, mine $223. He made his move. "How come his bill is $45 less than mine?" he said in his quiet voice, as if he were whispering in a cathedral. Nice guys like Garold whisper a lot.

The clerk looked stumped for a moment. I could see I would have to speak for Garold. "We both had rooms without hot water last night," I said to the desk clerk. "I complained. The night clerk said she would take $45 off my bill. You should take $45 off his bill, too."

"That's right," Garold said, again speaking barely above a whisper.

The clerk took $45 off his rate.

"Did you complain too?" Norma asked Garold when he told her they had reduced his bill.

"No. Tom complained for me," he said. "I just pointed out that his bill was less than mine and then let him do the talking."

And from that moment until this we have called him "Ditto Davis." His "be nice" policy, it seems, has a corollary: Hang out with a grump, and if he complains about something, just say "Ditto."

THE SATURDAY
NIGHT CLUB

When my mother turned eighty, my sister and I gave her a birthday party. "We can invite anyone you'd like," we said. "Let's have a really fun party."

"Oh," she said in her typical way, "I don't want anyone but just you kids. I don't want a big party."

We insisted. "We're going to have a party, so you might just as well invite some people you'd like to see. How about your friends? Which friends should we invite?"

She fought back. "I don't want any of those old people coming over here for a birthday party," she said. "Laws, they can't even get up the steps." She was referring to the three flights of stairs from the street to her house.

And that was that. A lot of family members and

younger friends came, but not old folks who couldn't climb the steps. If you want to age in style, you hang out with the young ones. That was Mom's philosophy.

She felt differently about going to the Alice Louise Reynolds Club and the Litralure Club [sic.], the members of which met monthly to review a book and have lunch together. She joined them when she was in her thirties or forties. It was okay then to be with older people—although she remembered her friends there as "girls." "Oh, she's a darling girl," she would say. I never understood the difference between meeting "darling girls" at club meetings and having them to your birthday party. She told Louise and me once how the conversations had changed over the years: "We used to talk about raising our children. Now we just talk about how hard it is to clip our toenails."

Conversations change as people age, no doubt about it, as do associations. My friend Kevin recorded his grandmother's description of the Saturday Night Club to which she belonged:

"There used to be fourteen of us, but seven died, so now there's only seven of us. And we meet at 8:00 and everyone's ready to go home by 10:00. Except Helen has heart fibrillations, so she goes home by 9:00. We used to meet every two weeks, but now we only meet every two months, because that's the only time we can get six together to play cards. But we still have a hard time at that, because Ann's husband died, and then she had a stroke. Gladys's husband died also, but she remarried Clark, and now they both have heart troubles.

"Well, we take turns meeting at each other's houses. Except Ruby said that if we meet at Gladys's house she can't come, because the steps don't have a railing. That's because Ruby has to use a walker, and so does her husband Bob; but Ruby can't get up steps without a railing so she can't get in Gladys's house. But Clark fixed it so that she can come in through the garage. So now we can go to Gladys's and we all go in through the garage.

"And when we go to Ruby's house there's always the fountain. Yes, we always see the fountain. When we walk in the house, Ruby says, 'You need to see the fountain,' and we all say, 'We've already seen the fountain.' And she says, 'Nope, you've got to see the fountain.' Then she goes and turns on the water to the pond and we all see the fountain. So we've been seeing the fountain for twenty years now.

"The Saturday Night Club used to travel to Sun Valley and other places. One year we rented a bus and drove down to Zion's. We go back and Bobo [her husband] learned that he drove the whole way and never got in high gear. Yep, drove the whole way and never got in high gear. Oh, and we always have the New Year's Eve party. Last year we had it at Helen's house. Except her husband, who has Alzheimer's, got out of the house. So we spent the whole night looking for Helen's husband.

"Well, the Saturday Night Club is in poor shape, I tell ya. And we can't learn new games. I wanted to teach 'em Head and Foot, but they're in too poor of shape. So that's the Saturday Night Club."

On reflection, I have to agree with my mother. I don't want a bunch of old people at my eightieth birthday party either. It's an oxymoron to have your nearly dead friends singing "Happy Birthday." Bring on the young folks.

PART 3

LAMENTATIONS AND DEFIANCE

"I don't trust my body anymore."

—FRIEND, IN HER FORTIES,
AFTER BREAST CANCER

*"You can't just sit around feeling
sorry for yourself."*

—ELVA, AGE NINETY

LIVING
WITH REALITY

When Louise announced thirty-three years ago that she wanted a singing canary to grace our apartment, her intentions escaped me. She has since explained to me with great patience, and I still may not have this just right, that she had seen a pretty bamboo bird cage in a shop window. The vision of a little yellow singing canary in that cage made her happy. It would add much to the atmosphere of our student apartment. A canary was just right, first, because, unlike parakeets that make a lot of racket, it would sing brightly, and second, unlike parakeets, it would not tear the bamboo cage apart. It would lighten the tiny space that Louise had transformed from remarkably ugly rooms and a filthy kitchen with maggots in the stove to an attractive student apartment.

That project had involved refinishing floors, painting walls and ceiling, installing white metal cabinets in
the kitchen, refinishing a round oak table (which we
bought for forty dollars over my protest), and purchas-
ing black bentwood chairs with cane seats and a red
carpet. I had shamelessly argued against the red carpet
because it replaced the mottled brown and green one
that a well-meaning carpet layer had given us for our
wedding. Louise had conspired from the first day to get
rid of it, and now, after several years of rug-hate, it was
gone.

I confess that I miss the rug even now. It was made
of Herculon, a fiber that had the quality of boondoggle,
those brightly colored plastic laces I used to weave into
chains for pocketknives when I was a Boy Scout.
Consequently, the carpet was nonporous, stain resistant, wear resistant, and impervious to roaches and
rodents. Cars made of Herculon could go for two mil-
lion miles without an oil change. Louise said it was as
ugly as squid and had to go. We sold it to an arriving
business-school student, who said it looked like a great
long-term investment.

So at Louise's urging we went shopping for a canary.
"I want to call it Elizabeth Ann," Louise said. "I'm so
excited. Elizabeth Ann. Don't you think that's a darling
name for a little singing canary? She will be our first
daughter." She clasped her hands tightly. The waltzing,

anapestic rhythms of the name "Elizabeth Ann," coupled with its innate femininity, eluded me.

At the Canary Store I asked the Canary Man if he had singing canaries. Now I recall a similar moment when my father asked a hotel desk clerk in Paris, "Parlez-vous Français?" Unlike the desk clerk, who politely said, "Oui," the Canary Man just tilted his head toward the back room. There on four walls, floor to ceiling, were dozens of little 10- by 10-inch cages, and in each one a brilliant yellow, orange, or mottled canary was singing its little lungs out.

"We want a good singer," I said to the man, who had followed us into the room.

He looked at me as if probing for signs of disorientation. "They're all good singers," he said. "They're singing canaries."

"Well," I said, "we want a female."

"We're going to name it Elizabeth Ann," Louise chimed in.

"The females don't sing," he said in a cold tone. "Only the males sing. I can't sell you a female singing canary. They don't exist. I can sell you a female that doesn't sing."

Louise looked crestfallen.

"Do you still want one?" I asked.

"Oh, yeah," she said. "We might as well. It will be

pretty, anyway. Let's get that little yellow one." I could tell her vision had lost some of its luster.

We climbed into the car with our new bright yellow canary chirping in its little cardboard box with air holes around the sides and the aesthetically appealing bamboo bird cage that Louise had spotted in the front window of the store. We drove for a while in silence.

I broke the silence. "His name will be Fang."

"Oh, geez," she said.

And Fang it was. I don't know if it was the name that turned him off or the anti-male-canary environment that pervaded our living room. Fang quit singing on the second day. When we went on vacation once, we had the Canary Man board him for a few days. When we picked him up, he was singing. Again he quit on the second day.

Our photograph, taken on the day that we arrived home, with Louise smiling brightly beside the bird cage, is an out-and-out fraud. Fang was a disappointment. He had failed as an *objet d'art* and he was a lousy pet, flailing wildly around his cage when anyone approached. His failure made him my bird. Louise wanted nothing to do with him. He was just another guy in the house who didn't sing.

What's more, he soon became the focus of my daily attentions, not by choice but by necessity. He was becoming ill. I noticed one day that one of his little talons had turned black and fallen off.

"Oh my gosh, that's really ugly," Louise said. Thereafter she avoided Fang and his bamboo cage entirely.

I took him to the Angell Memorial Pet Clinic in Boston and waited patiently with him there, fending off an English setter that desperately wanted to bird-dog him, only to hear from a sympathetic veterinarian, "Unfortunately, veterinary medicine just doesn't know a whole lot about bird ailments yet." She patted my arm like I've seen funeral directors do.

I took Fang home, gave him fresh food and water, and cleaned his cage. A second talon turned black and fell off. And a third. Finally I took the hapless Fang, who was now lurching around on stumps on the bottom of his cage because his talons were entirely gone and he could not sit on his perch, to a different vet and insisted that something be done. He shrugged his shoulders. "You might try changing his diet," he said. "Try giving him some popcorn." Popcorn. That was it? Popcorn? His bill for the visit was thirty-five dollars.

One morning I awoke to silence. Fang was not thumping around as usual. I found him on his back, stumps up. I gently put him in a brown lunch bag and buried him at the corner of the apartment building just behind the sandbox. Then I went to Louise, who was still in bed.

"Fang died," I said. "I buried him out by the sand-box." My voice broke. Louise held me for a while until I felt better. She didn't cry, though.

Although the aesthetics of our lives still figure prominently in our daily conversations, we have become more and more like Fang. We talk about our aches and pains, examine our bodies for warts and moles, and mourn the loss of our sleek figures and smooth skin. Louise has had one ankle fused and had surgery to repair a collapsed lung. I have had surgery on a torn cartilage in my right knee and on a brain tumor. We are not yet at Fang's late stages of lurching around, but we can see that possibility down the road.

We have become realistic hypochondriacs. It makes Louise nervous to feel pain in her good lung. I go to the doctor when I get a headache.

"It feels strange," I said to him recently. "The pain begins on top of my head, winds around the back, and ends in my right eyeball."

He patted my arm, just as the veterinarian once did, and said, "The psychology of tumors is very powerful."

So along with conversations about decorating and accessories, we now spend a lot of time talking about our not-too-slowly aging bodies. On any given day one or the other of us has ovarian cancer, brain cancer, or early Alzheimer's. Our bodies are simply not to be trusted anymore. Only the young and deluded trust their bodies.

We have read books that make it all worse. In an unthinking moment when she thought she might write a novel about a woman with cancer, Louise bought *Everyone's Guide to Cancer Therapy*. It's hypochondriac heaven. Just at random I opened the book to a chapter titled "Living with an Ostomy." It lists three: colostomy, ileostomy, and urostomy. There's a section on bone marrow and blood stem cell transplantation, one on controlling pain, and on and on, enough chapters to make even healthy people feel malignant.

It's easier to win the lottery than to avoid trouble. The book explains that "our chromosomes contain millions of different messages that tell the body how it should grow, function, and behave." There are, it continues, "an incredible number of genes and an unimaginable number of messages. And since the chromosomes reproduce themselves every time a cell divides, there are lots of opportunities for something to go wrong."

If I just think about the messages Louise and I send back and forth on any given day and how many of them get lost or misunderstood, then the odds for one of the trillion messages that my chromosomes are shooting back and forth through my body to be misunderstood are staggering. And when a message goes awry, you don't get a notice on your computer screen to signal a system error. It just goes merrily on its way, doubling, ever doubling, raising havoc everywhere it happens to land until one day you get a sudden back pain or double vision or bleeding from your ears.

I conclude, against all of my youthful instincts, that my body is a terminal illness. I asked my friend Francine Bennion, who has dealt with her diabetes since childhood, "What's the upside of my pituitary tumor, Francine?"

She looked me squarely in the eye and said without flinching, "Now you can begin to live in reality."

A Lament for Two Aging Voices

The following is a recitation to be done preferably by two people in their mid-fifties or older. Speak together or separately as the lines indicate (bold type shows voices together in unison):

1st Voice	2nd Voice
Oh, doctor,	
	Oh, doctor,
hear my plea.	
	hear my plight.
My medical handbook	**My medical handbook**
is stuffed	
	cover to cover
cover to cover	**cover to cover**

1ST VOICE	2ND VOICE
with old age delights	
	with old age blights
blights	**blights**
beginning with A	
	and ending with Z.
It lists without mercy,	It lists without mercy
what's waiting for me.	**what's waiting for me.**
A is for	
	anemia
amnesia	aphasia
Alzheimer's	**Alzheimer's**
	What did you say?
arthritis	aneurism
and	atrial
fibrillation	rillation
rillation	rillation

1st Voice	2nd Voice
	B is for
back pain	
	bedsores
bloating	
	and bowlegs
(not good for a dancer)	**(not good for a dancer)**
then blood	
	pressure
	blood
clots	
brain tumors	**brain tumors**
breast cancer	**breast cancer**
C is for	
	chest pain
colitis and	
	chronic fatigue
I'm always tired	**I'm always tired**
and constipation	
	beats fibrillation
or cardiac arrest	
	arrest
arrest	
	arrest.

1ST VOICE	2ND VOICE
	D is for
deafness	decay
and depression	**and depression**
	diabetes
dementia	dysphasia
and	
duo-	**duo-**
denum	**denum**
obstructions	**obstructions**
to be	**to be**
deconstructed	**deconstructed**
E is for	
	embolism
emphysema	
I can hardly breathe	**I can hardly breathe**
	edema
and please don't fight us	**and please don't fight us**
pass the Gas-X	
erosive gastritis	**erosive gastritis**

1st Voice	2nd Voice
	F is for
forgetfulness	
	Where are we?
In "F" as in fractures	
	and, oh yes, fatigue
G is for	
	gallstones
glaucoma	
	and golfer's dystonia
poor baby	**poor baby**
and gout	
Good grief!	**Good grief!**
	H is for
hemorrhoids	
	halitosis
and hair loss	
Big deal!	**Big deal!**
	Try the hypos and hypers—
like hypercholesterolemia	
	or hypoglycemia

1ST VOICE	2ND VOICE
hypo hyper	**hypo hyper**
hypo hyper	**hypo hyper**
Let's call the whole	**Let's call the whole**
thing off	**thing off**
I is for	
	infarctions
infections	
	and inflammations
insulin	
	excess
	and
insulin	
	insufficiency
It all makes me tense	
	and, yeah, impotence.
	J is for
joint disorders	
	That's it? Not even a
	rhyme?
We don't have time.	
K is for	
	kidney

1ST VOICE	2ND VOICE
stones	
kidney	
	failure
	kidney
cancer	
No kidding around	**No kidding around**
	L is for
lousy luck	
	meaning liver
cancer	
	liver
failure	
Lou Gehrig's disease	**Lou Gehrig's disease**
	lymphoma
I wanna go homah!	
M is for	
	melanoma
menopause	
	memory
loss	
	Henry lost what?
metabolic disorders	
	and myasthenia

<u>1ST VOICE</u>	<u>2ND VOICE</u>
gravis	**gravis**
	N stands for
narcolepsy	
	a tiresome thing, and
neurological disorders	
	That covers a lot.
Yes, it does if you've got 'em	
	from stem to stern
from top to bottom **from bottom to top.**	**from top to bottom** **from bottom to top.**
O stands for	
	osteo-stuff
Like osteo-what?	
	Like osteoarthritis
And osteoporosis	
I'm bending already	**I'm bending already**
Then on to ovarian cancer,	
a bad one for sure. **But we're looking for** **cures.**	**a bad one for sure.** **But we're looking for** **cures.**

1ST VOICE	2ND VOICE
	P is for
P is a long one	
	But skip it we can't
So what are you saying?	
	Get on with the chant.
Well, there's pain	
	and palsy
and palpitations.	
	Then Parkinson's and
pancreatic cancer **I'm glad we're past** **that one**	**pancreatic cancer** **I'm glad we're past** **that one**
	and platelet dysfunction.
Pneumonia, the old folks' friend,	
	pneumothorax
I hate p-n-e-u's	
	But we're still not through
There's poly-	
	myalgia rheumatica, a long one for sure, and poly-
arthritis nodosa.	
	I know a Polly.

1ST VOICE	2ND VOICE
A Polly Nodosa?	
	No, a Polly Spinoza.
Not the same one.	
	And prostate cancer
That's hard on a fencer.	
	And pulmonary cysts and pulmonary
embolism.	
And that's not symbolism.	**And that's not symbolism.**
Q is for	
	Quaking.
Quaking. That's it?	
	That's it. But quaking's no fun at all
No, it's no fun at all	
	'cause it feels like ants
deep inside your pants.	**deep inside your pants.**
	R is for
rectal	
	cancer rectal
bleeding	

1ST VOICE	2ND VOICE
not receding	**not receding**
	retina
degeneration	
	and a couple of rheumas
Pumas?	
	No, rheumas.
	Like rheuma-
tism	
and rheuma-	
	toid
and her friend Arthur	
	Arthur?
Yep, Arthur Itis.	
S is for	
	Sadness.
That's everyone's yoke.	
	Then sarcomas
and shin splints	
	and please don't forget
strokes, folks.	**strokes, folks.**
Eat yer veggies and	**Eat yer veggies and**
fruits.	**fruits.**
But they'll stick in your	
throats, folks,	

1ST VOICE	2ND VOICE
	yes, they'll stick in your throats,
if you've got a thing	
	if you've got a thing
called a Schatzki's ring.	**called a Schatzki's ring.**
And one last s-word I don't want to say.	
	This one last s-word We just have to say.
On Dancer, on Prancer,	
	On Prancer, on Dancer,
It's stomach cancer.	**It's stomach cancer.**
	T is for
Tired. I'm tired of this I'm getting depressed	
	But we have to get through
we have to get through	
before we can sleep	**before we can sleep**
	So now I re-peep:
	T is for
tachycardia	

1ST VOICE	2ND VOICE
	ventricular
tachycardia	
	atrial
thrombosis	
	thrombosis and just three more:
tremors	**tremors**
trots and	**trots and**
tumors galore	**tumors galore**
U is for	
	ulcers,
and ureth-	
	ritis and urinary
in-	
	continence.
Incontinence.	
	A wet one for sure.
And for uterine cancer	And for uterine cancer
there might be a cure.	**there might be a cure.**
	V is for
Very—I'm very tired.	
	No, vari- as in varicose veins.

1ST VOICE	2ND VOICE
	Now get moving, get busy
But I'm getting dizzy. There's vertigo	
	yes, vertigo and voice box cancer
And of course we all pray for Alice's	
	Yes, we'll all pray for her
voice box paralysis.	**voice box paralysis.**
W is for	
	a short list for sure.
Here we won't camp.	
	No here we won't camp. There's warts
and wrinkles	
and writer's cramp.	**and writer's cramp.**
	X is for
xanthelasthma	
	Xanthel what?
Xanthelasthma.	
	Xanthel-asthma?

1ST VOICE	2ND VOICE
You heard it just right.	
	I'm glad I don't have it.
It's a terrible blight.	**It's a terrible blight.**
Y is for	
	Yippee skippee, we're almost through
Not yippee skippee— for yips and yaws	
	yaws and yips
Yup.	**Yup.**
	Z we include
'Cause we have to have Z	
To round out the list.	**To round out the list.**
	The word is zoster.
Zoster?	
	Yes, zoster
And we'll tell you anyhow	
	Yes, we'll promise you now,

1ST VOICE	2ND VOICE
	We won't make a roster
No, we won't make a roster	
Listing old folks with zoster.	**Listing old folks with zoster.**

WIN-WIN, WIN-LOSE, LOSE-WIN, LOSE-LOSE

When our sons first married and occasionally came home to complain about their wives, they found no sympathy from us. We knew marriage becomes better when you struggle with hard stuff together and survive it. Almost anyone can survive Disneyland—if you stay away from Space Mountain. Surviving teenagers and depression and fears by the potful—that makes marriage better.

I once thought—not even too long ago—that I had the whole thing figured out. I had already lived through the towels-on-the-floor years, the toothpaste-cap-stuck-in-the-drain years, the this-salmon-is-rotten-and-I'm-not-going-to-eat-it years. Yes, we'd had our fights in earlier days, and we have our disagreements now, but we know how to communicate.

"Live with it," I said to my sons when they fretted over their marital trials. "Learn to love her not *in spite* of her foibles but precisely *because* of her foibles." And I'd stick out my chest and give them my best listen-to-what-I-say-I-am-the-omniscient-family-patriarch look. Of course I've never let them read my journal entry written in Vienna in July 1997:

This morning in Vienna I am looking for the nail clippers. It is important not to lose nail clippers in a foreign country, because sometimes they are hard to replace, and even if they aren't hard to replace, it's hard to find a specialty store that stocks them. It's not like going into any supermarket or drugstore in America and voilà—nail clippers. In Austria, pharmacies sell pharmaceutical items, grocery stores sell groceries, and Bipa—that's the name of the franchise, Bipa—sells cosmetics, shampoo, and, not least of all, nail clippers. Keeping facts like this straight is essential for your mental health. If you go into Bipa and ask for aspirin, you will get a very dirty look from a sales clerk who has learned how to scowl at foreign customers. "We don't have aspirin here," she says, and her tone adds, without her saying the words, "stupid meathead jerk."

So I am looking for the nail clippers not only so I can trim my nails, which have become long and jagged, but to preserve my mental health. And this is not the first time I've looked for nail clippers in Vienna. I couldn't find them the last time I wanted to use them, either. I asked Louise, and she produced them from her bedroom drawer. I put them away in a drawer in the bathroom that we both use. "Let's keep them in the bathroom," I said. "That way we can both find them." She didn't answer. And now they are not in the drawer in the bathroom.

I want to rage, "Where in the heck are the nail clippers, Laweeeeze!?" but I keep my mouth shut, because my body language as I now storm around the apartment is saying more than enough. I don't yell, because every time I do I have to apologize. I have to apologize for yelling, and I have to apologize for being wrong when she finds them in the bathroom right under my nose.

I try to reconstruct the past. Maybe I put them in my drawer in the bedroom. I clipped my nails while sitting on the bed and dropped trimmings into the wastebasket. Did I put them in my drawer? I search my drawer, lifting out underwear, looking under socks and removing those with holes as I go. I could write a history of the family as seen through holey socks.

"Louise," I ask, "do you know where the nail clippers are?"

"Yes, they're in the top drawer of my chest."

"I thought we were going to keep them in the bathroom drawer."

No answer.

"Louise?"

Silence.

"I'm not going to win this one, am I?"

"Yes," she says, "just keep them in the top drawer of my chest, and you'll win."

I consider it one of the paradoxes of marriage. Do I win by winning, win by losing, lose by winning, or lose by losing? It took me many years to learn that I might actually win more ground by losing than by trying to win.

But I can't let go of it. So while we are eating our Austrian supper of hard rolls, ham, and cheese in Vienna on lost-nail-clipper day I ask Louise, "What do you think about the struggle of marriage? Do we win by winning, win by losing, lose by winning, or lose by losing?"

She looks at me hard, like I am weird, and continues to chew. After she swallows, she says, "How did you come up with that?"

It's always a bad sign when she asks that, because it means I'm not going to hide behind my philosophical mask. She's going to rip it off and expose me to daylight. "It's just a question," I say. "Do we win by winning, win by losing, lose by winning, or lose by losing?"

"No, that's not just a question," she says. "What's the story behind the question?"

So I confess that I've been thinking about the lost nail clippers and repeat the questions.

"Well," she says, "in your case, you win by losing, and in my case I win by winning." And she lets out one of her big healthy laughs.

After a few moments, she says, "Actually, Tom, the last time you had your nail clippers in the bathroom drawer, you couldn't see them. You kept looking in there, and if they'd been a dog, they'd have bitten you."

She borrowed that phrase from my mother, who used to send me off to look for things I couldn't find, even though they were right in front of me. When I reported that I couldn't find whatever I was supposed to retrieve, she'd say. "It's right there. If it'd been a dog it would have bitten you."

"So now," Louise was playing her trump card, "they're in my drawer, and you can find them in there. And you've won after all."

Louise: win-win

Tom: lose-win

Of course there have been lose-lose situations in our marriage, but nothing in our recent or distant past years has been so nasty as the fight I once read about between a magician and his wife. They had a ferocious argument, and he stormed out of the house. She in turn retrieved his magic bunny from its cage, the one he pulled out of the hat in performances, Flopsy, to whom he'd become quite attached. She wrung its neck, skinned it, cleaned it, and served it up to him in a prune sauce. When he said it was a delicious dish, asked what it was and could he have seconds, she told him he had just eaten Flopsy, and yes, he could have seconds.

Wife: win-win

Husband: lose-lose

Rabbit: lose-lose

And while the thought of killing a pet revolts me most of the time, and while no one in our family has ever killed a pet—a real pet—to eat it, I recall a time when Louise and I did approach the line in scheming how to divide two lobsters among five people. We were in Minneapolis. The year was 1980. We were broke. But when we passed an aquarium of live lobsters in a supermarket, lobsters that were on sale for three dollars apiece, we could not pass them by. Our minds drifted back to our years in Boston, when we would go down to the lobster pound on the wharf, pick out some two-pounders, take them home, boil them up, and snarf them down with melted butter. Our Pavlovian responses kicked in, and we decided on the spot that two lobsters for six dollars were not to be passed over.

"What about the boys?" Louise said.

"What about the boys?" I said.

She was referring to our sons, Jonathan, Edmund, and Charles, who were drifting around the candy department fingering the Gummi Bears.

"They have to eat too," she said.

"We'll cook them up some hot dogs," I said. "They won't want lobster."

"But they should learn to eat lobster," Louise said. "It's one of the fine things of life."

"I don't want to share mine with anyone," I said, "and I'm not going to buy another one."

I knew what to do. When we got home with the lobsters, I took them out of the bag. "Hey, guys, look what we got. Lobsters."

"Cool," one of them said. "What do you do with them?"

"Well, you can race them," I said. "Let's name them and have a race on the kitchen floor. This one's Harry and this one's Larry. Which one do you think can move faster?"

Ed: "Harry."

Jon: "Larry."

Charles: "Gross."

Charles was the youngest of our sons and the most easily repelled by creatures resembling giant roaches. He wouldn't want lobster anyway. He was not going to be a problem here.

"Okay, Jon, you cheer for Larry, and Ed, you cheer for Harry. Ready. Go."

And the lobster race was on. Two or three races.

"But now it's time to cook Harry and Larry and eat 'em," I said.

"Huh? You're gonna cook 'em?"

"Yeah, lobster's great. You can have some of mine."

"Nu-uh, I don't want any."

"Me either."

So I boiled up the water with some salt, plunged the lobsters in head first, making little squealing sounds as I did so, "Yeaow, ow, oh my gosh, we're gonna die," that sort of thing. And Louise and I ate them undisturbed. The boys were perfectly happy with hot dogs.

Tom and Louise: win-win

Boys: lose-win

Larry and Harry: lose-lose

The tossed salad for Sunday dinner a few years ago, however, was a different matter. I take my tossed salads seriously. Everything gets tossed in: three kinds of lettuce, spinach, olives, artichoke hearts, zucchini, yellow squash, carrots, mushrooms, sunflower seeds, purple cabbage, and anything else in the produce department that appeals. My working principle is: colorful and abundant. A good salad takes me an hour and a half to make, shredding, chopping, cleaning up. This particular salad filled a huge bowl, and in my mind, this was enough for Sunday and several more days of healthy eating.

I turned my back from the salad for a moment. As I turned back around, Louise was pouring a bottle of Italian dressing all over my creation. It would not last beyond this meal. In an hour, the whole thing would be a wilted, stinking mess.

"What are you doing with my salad?" I was yelling. I was not being diplomatic.

"I'm putting on the salad dressing," Louise responded. Her voice was snappy, biting.

"I wanted to let everyone put on their own dressing," I snapped back. "Now the whole salad is ruined."

"That's just stupid," Louise said. "You can't toss salad on your salad plate. You have to toss salad before it's served. No one likes to dress their own salad." We were eyeball to eyeball, tooth to jowl. I didn't care what the children heard or thought. For years Louise had been drilling a principle into the inner recesses of my brain: Stay out of my business. Now she had meddled in mine. My chest throbbed with righteous indignation.

Louise walked into the living room. "Dinner's ready," she announced. "And Tom has made a delicious salad."

Tom: lose-lose

Louise: win-win

Our son Charles, who witnessed the spat, had just returned from a trip to San Francisco with his high school group. He told one of his friends that he had been away just a week, the family was happy when he left, and when he got back he thought his parents were getting a divorce. Over a salad.

Wrong. By the next Sunday, we had it figured out. I would fix a big salad, toss what was needed for the guests, and put the rest in the refrigerator.

Tom: win-win

Louise: win-win

Louise and I agree on one thing: Nothing is so satisfying as to win one over our sons and their friends. Driving back to Vienna from lower Austria with Sam and Jared Wright—his friend and ours—after a day of sightseeing, we passed through mountainous countryside. The road hugged steep, grassy hillsides where cows were grazing. They seemed to have no trouble at all staying up there, although one might wonder what kept them from losing their footing and rolling down onto the road.

"Did you know they breed those cows with the legs on one side shorter than the legs on the other so they can stay on the hills?" Louise asked.

"Huh," Sam said.

"No kidding," Jared said. "What happens if they turn the other way?"

Louise and I managed to stuff our laughter for just a few seconds before exploding.

"Chalk one up for the adults," Jared said. "Please don't tell my dad I fell for that."

Adults: win-win

Kids: lose-lose

AD NAUSEUM

From time to time I'll put everything on the line just to see if I can still do something I used to do. Usually this involves some kind of risk. Sometimes I do it because I don't want to be called chicken, but mostly I'm trying to prove I'm not old yet.

The day after our thirty-fifth wedding anniversary, we were in Caribou River, Nova Scotia, with our friends Norma and Garold, all of us past middle age, and Louise announced that she wanted to go to the fair. "It's in Trenton," she said. "It'll be fun."

Garold wanted to know what kind of fair it was going to be.

"I don't know," Louise said. "It's either an arts and crafts fair, where they exhibit all kinds of local work, or it's one of those cheapo carnival fairs where they have ex-convicts running the rides."

"I remember those in Provo," Norma said. "I took my grandkids, but I didn't let them out of my sight."

We piled into the car about 11:00 A.M. and headed out.

"First let's go to the poo-dee-doo shops in Pictou," Louise said, being a woman who had a vision of how the day was to go.

"What's poo-dee-doo?" Garold wanted to know.

"Oh, that's what Al and Ginny call those little home craft shops with all the knickknacks that you buy on vacation and wish you hadn't when you get them home."

"Kitsch," Norma said.

We drifted into two fine poo-dee-doo shops in Pictou, where I bought a teensy book of Robert Burns's poetry and a diary with loons on the cover. Garold and I had been quoting lines from Robert Burns to each other—he liked "To a Mouse," I liked "To a Louse" ("Ha, whar ya gaun ye crowlin ferlie?"). My dad used to recite Robert Burns's poems at parties of the local Scottish Society. I heard him recite "To a Louse" once in a church meeting, and even then, at eight years of age, I sensed my father's heretical leanings, although the moral base of the last stanza escaped me at that age:

> *O wad some Power the giftie gie us*
> *To see oursels as ithers see us!*
> *It wad frae monie a blunder free us,*

An' foolish notion:
What airs in dress an' gait wad lea'e us,
An ev'n devotion.

After we were poo-dee-dooed out, we strolled over
to Fougeres, a restaurant owned by a Swiss family. We
each had a bowl of seafood chowder, followed by apple
strudel and banana cream pie. I left room for a caramel-
pecan ice cream cone. Louise caved in and bought a
chocolate cone to add to her banana cream pie.

Now filled with chowder, fat, and sugar, we headed
for Trenton. Even from two blocks away I knew this
was not going to be an arts and crafts fair. There were
too many cars, too much noise, too many children and
teenagers. Then the clattering and grinding of the rides
became audible.

"Oh, goody," Louise said, clasping her hands. "I
want to go on the Tilt-a-Whirl. I love the Tilt-a-Whirl.
Will you go on the Tilt-a-Whirl with me, Garold?"

"No," Garold said. His one-syllable answer left little room for doubt.

For the uninitiated, I should explain that the Tilt-a-
Whirl is a carnival ride invented by Satan. It's not one
of the loop-the-loop rides that turns you upside down
and dumps your brains on the pavement below. And it's
not like the Ferris wheel, where your brains and your
stomach trade places. The Tilt-a-Whirl is more subtle.
It spins your brains out by centrifugal force. It looks

like something people who are afraid of the monster, soaring rides could go on and survive. It is just a cut above the merry-go-round, the prospective rider might think. And thus the seductive finger of a demon beckons and a little voice whispers, "Come to me. It's fun. Come to me."

The machine consists of a group of little compartments shaped like beach cabanas on rollers mounted on a big platform that serpentines up and down in a circle while the little compartments, each holding up to four riders, twirl around. Hence, it tilts and it twirls, "tilt" and "twirl," innocent words that conjure images of little dancing girls.

"Will you go on the Tilt-a-Whirl with me?" Louise asked, tugging on my sleeve.

Normally I cave in to almost anything Louise wants, but I remembered the last time I was on a Tilt-a-Whirl. I had returned from Germany that morning. I was sleeping soundly to the point of jet-lag death when Louise woke me with a sharp, "Tom, get up. We're going to the fair at Provo High."

I rolled over and groaned, my head spinning, and said there was no way I'd go to a fair that afternoon.

"Get up," she said in her most shovey voice. It was a tone she reserved for special occasions.

I groaned.

"Come on, don't be a party poop. Get up."

If I'd had the manhood I should have exhibited, I'd have refused. But I struggled off the bed, pulled on my shoes, and lumbered to the car.

"I'll drive," Louise said efficiently.

I don't remember much about the fair. There was a lot of earsplitting music, rude kids bumping against my numb body, and my son's hand out asking for more money.

"C'mon," Louise said, "we're going on the Tilt-a-Whirl."

I was too dazed to think. I stumbled into the waiting cabana. I remember only a few of the details after that—spinning wildly, feeling like I was going to throw up, wanting to throw up, not being able to throw up, Louise laughing hysterically. Then it was over. I stumbled off, told Louise I was nauseated, that I absolutely had to go home, and remembered nothing more until noon the next day.

So my answer as our car steered inexorably toward Trenton this afternoon was, "No way. I will not go on the Tilt-a-Whirl with you."

I dropped Louise, Norma, and Garold off at the park entrance and parked the car. When I found them again, they were standing next to the Tilt-a-Whirl.

"C'mon," Louise said. "Garold won't go with me. I've got two tickets."

Why didn't I say, "Phooey on you. You go twice"?

Why didn't I say, "Tough, you just wasted the money"?
I know why. It's because my mother brought me up as a
member of the "Clean-Plate Club," which meant you
always ate everything on your plate, even if you felt like
exploding. Being a member of the Clean-Plate Club
meant you wasted nothing. Not food. Not clothing.
And especially not money. Louise had bought the
tickets. My honorary presidency of the Clean-Plate
Club, bestowed by my doting mother and earned at no
small cost in childhood, dictated that I must use the
ticket.

Besides, I might have subconsciously wanted to
prove I could still be champ at the amusement park. I
climbed up the ramp and waited for our turn on the
devil twirler. I hardly noticed that the average age of the
other riders was about ten years old, and that no other
people within forty-seven and a half years of my age
were getting on. Then the ride stopped, and we found
our own death-cabana right next to the operator, a
reddish-haired, grinning Nova Scotian.

"Are you ready for this?" he asked. His smile was
too friendly, too gleeful.

He locked the security bar around us and the riders
in other cabanas. Norma and Garold stood looking on.
Norma took our picture. I think I made some incredi-
bly stupid comment like, "This is a picture of Tom and
Louise just before they died."

The first rotation was not bad, not bad at all. "I can do this," I thought. "It's a kiddie ride." On the second rotation our cabana went into a really mean spin, but only one. "I really can do this," I thought. "I'm going to live through this." After that the spinning seemed unceasing. Wild, head-jerking convulsions. Round and round she goes. I wanted to throw up. I knew I would throw up.

Louise was laughing hysterically. Then she was yelling, "I'm going to wet my pants." Then, after a few more rounds, "He's trying to kill us."

On each successive round I caught a glimpse of Beelzebub the Operator. He was casually talking to a buddy. He showed no intention of shutting off the ride. When he watched us go by on one rotation, pale and drained of life, he smiled. He was indeed trying to kill us.

Finally I saw his finger reach for the shut-off button. The machine ground to a stop.

As Louise and I staggered off, she asked him, "What did you do? You did something."

He grinned broadly. "I released your brakes," he said.

I stumbled over to a concession booth and bought a 7-Up. We sipped on it. "That's enough," Louise said. "I've had my ride. We can go now."

Somehow I managed to drive the car to the grocery

store, where we needed to pick up a few things for dinner. On the way, Norma said consoling things like "That's too bad. That's just too bad."

Garold was making smarty cracks like "Would you like a frank and beans? How about a corn dog?"

"Shut up, Garold," Louise, Norma, and I said almost in unison.

Partway down the first grocery aisle Louise said, "I've got to go back to the car. I'm going to throw up." She took a plastic grocery bag and left. I managed to stay in the store to assist Norma and Garold in the shopping, but from time to time the ground seemed to shift under my feet, and I was overcome with nausea all over again.

It wasn't until a couple of hours after returning home, after sitting on the beach inhaling fresh sea air, that I began to feel that I might live long enough to refuse to tilt and whirl again.

But Louise, who had also recovered, said, "I don't think I've been on my last Tilt-a-Whirl ride yet."

To demonstrate that we are not the only crazy old people on the planet, I share an account sent to me by my friend Al, who is my age, just three weeks before the Tilt-a-Whirl debacle. He titled it "Another fine mess you've gotten me into now, Ollie":

Dear Tom,

The subject is the theme of our Memorial Day outing.

It seems every time we go somewhere with Kristy [a daughter in her early twenties] we get into some kind of pickle. The time we were caught in a flash flood in the Zion Narrows comes to mind.

This time we decided at the last minute to see what the deal is with the Grand Staircase Escalante National Monument. There are not many facilities, not many camp-grounds, but one of the motels in Boulder had a cancellation, so we took it. We were pleasantly surprised to find a very neat, clean motel, with only twelve rooms. Ours had two queen beds. For forty-nine dollars per night, it was not much more expensive than camping.

We looked at the brochures and decided on a hike to Calf Creek Falls, described as moderately strenuous. We poo-pooed that as we started out with our water, but we walked forever, even though it was only 2.75 miles each way. That turned out to be about 2.0 miles too much each way. I simply was not used to that kind of walking in the sun and heat to boot. When we got there, though, there was a spectacular falls about 130 feet high with a large pool under it and the coldest water imaginable. We waded in it as much as we could to anesthetize our aching feet. On the way out, Ginny and I agreed it was indeed a moderately strenuous hike. Our legs were very sore, and I didn't think I would ever walk again. Kristy, of course, could have done it on her hands.

So naturally, the next day we went to the ranger

station in Escalante to find some kind of easier thing to do. They recommended the slot canyons called Peek-a-boo and Spooky Gulch. Sounded like a piece of cake, as long as it wasn't raining.

To get to the trailhead, we had to travel thirty miles on a dirt road, washboard much of the way. When we got there, there was a switchback trail down to the bottom of Dry Coyote Gulch, some five to seven hundred feet. When we got to Peek-a-boo Slot Canyon, we saw clearly that it was not a piece of cake. The words of the cashier at the local store in Boulder bounced around in my deaf head: "It isn't necessarily a good thing, this monument business. For example, the local search-and-rescue team wanted to stage a training evacuation including a life-flight helicopter. They couldn't do it. Now that it is a monument, no helicopter is allowed to land, not even for rescues. So be real careful in there, folks. We don't even have an ambulance."

The entrance to the slot canyon from the bottom required using shallow, poorly placed handholds and footholds to climb up a sheer wall of sandstone about twenty feet. (I would have thought thirty feet at first look.) As luck would have it, some people we knew from our neighborhood came out. They struggled quite a bit to get down. They were younger and fitter.

Ginny said she had already had enough and was going to the car when our neighbor, his wife, and his daughter insisted we had to go, absolutely, positively. They also said it would be much easier to climb up and go through the slot from the bottom, not from the top down. Under protest, Ginny was dragged to the face of the thing and goaded into starting off. Kristy went up first, of course, without any problem. Our neighbor pushed Ginny up, and she finally, after a lot of effort, got up to a narrow ledge, and then had to do it all over again to get over the last ten feet. Then he pushed me up.

Once we were up there, it was clear that we wouldn't be able to go down the way we had gone up. Trapped, we started climbing in the slot. Every six to ten feet there would be another wall we had to get over, about four feet high. There would be no foot- or handholds, so by flopping, flailing, and pushing with knees and elbows and hands, we would heave our old carcasses somehow up the four feet, only to find another such obstacle another few feet away.

By the fourth or fifth such effort, we were exhausted, scraped up, bruised up. It was clear that this would not work. At about the same spot there were others, much younger and fitter, who had reached the same conclusion. We were well and truly trapped, unable to go on, afraid to go back. Kristy went on in an exploring effort and returned saying that the slot went on and up for a long ways and got tighter, requiring climbing through a hole and sucking it in to get around a bend. I could see myself sucking it in only to wedge myself like Pooh at Rabbit's house, waiting *to lose enough weight to get out, or waiting for a good rainstorm to explode me out like a cork in a dam. She said we definitely didn't want to go on.*

Since it was such a cool place with water-sculpted walls, arches above us, and other fantastic formations (although rather tight and claustrophobia generating), we decided to wait where we were and let Kristy go on, have fun, and explore for about twenty minutes, when she would return and we would formulate a plan. Actually she went to the top and back again in twenty-five minutes.

Our plan was simple. We would slide our aching and scratched corpses down these ledges until we got to the final drop, and then we would worry about the last descent. When we got there, it seemed like fifty feet. There was simply no way. Just then, a climber guy with ropes and a harness and other equipment appeared and offered to help us down. Kristy, for the fun of it, put the rope around herself and rappelled down without effort. Then they put Ginny in the harness and gradually lowered her with the help of the foot- and handholds. She got down without any trouble that way. Next it was my turn. I knew that the harness would not fit me. Not close. No way. I didn't want the embarrassment of trying it on only to give up with the obvious conclusion that I was too fat.

Then I got mad. How could I be so old, out of shape, and fat? The anger brought a shot of testosterone and adrenaline. "Clear out of the way," I shouted authorita-

tively, "I'm coming down." I was going to do it myself. I didn't care if I landed as a pile of compressed lard at the bottom. There was quite a crowd by now. The first ten feet or so, I slid on my behind with my heels catching the little footholds and breaking my descent enough to get me to the first ledge. I started to do the same with the last ten feet when the rope guy said that he thought I should turn around and do it the other way. I said, "Nah, I'm okay this way." Two or three quick moves with the feet into the footholds and I jumped the last four feet, landing on the soft sand on the bottom.

"Well," said the rope guy, "good job." What was unsaid hung in the air like a cloudburst. Everyone was thinking it. (" . . . for a fat old dork.") Even if he had said it, I would have taken it as a compliment, because never before in my life have I ever felt more like a fat old dork. That did it for the slot canyons, and we heaved our aching, bruised bodies out of Coyote Dry Gulch and left. We never did make it to Spooky Gulch. Going on trips with Kristy is always interesting and exciting.

Thought you might like to know.

Al

I asked Gene, a second friend, to write about his bicycle accident. He never responded. His wife e-mailed me back under the title, "It isn't funny." Sorry, Dorothy. But isn't it a teensy bit amusing to hear about someone stretched backwards over the wheels and frame of his bike in the gravel, waiting for an ambulance, while another guy tells the crowd gathered around about his bike accident at the same spot the year before, and his black Labrador is licking the helpless biker's face?

Why do any of us risk life and limb in such ventures? I think it's because we're trying to prove that we can still run with the young'uns, that we're still alive. My mother, when she could barely see, baked a batch of cookies every week just to see if she could still do it. That was all the risk she could handle, but it sufficed.

I'm with Louise, I guess. I don't think I've been on my last Tilt-a-Whirl ride yet.

Beware the
Kindly Doctor

When I was a child, my family had a kindly doctor. He had grandfatherly white hair and a trimmed mustache, a steady, sympathetic gaze, and an air of confidence that put me entirely at ease. This was a man to be trusted. Hadn't I seen his likeness countless times on Norman Rockwell's covers of the *Saturday Evening Post?* Dr. Dunno was the archetypal Wise Old Man become flesh. He seemed as magical as Santa Claus. When anyone in the family became ill, we called Dr. Dunno, and he came, it seemed to me, as quickly as any doctor retrieves patients from the waiting room. I imagined him sitting by his phone with a concerned look on his face, day in and day out, waiting for our family to call so he could rush to our bedsides.

My earliest memory is of being in his care. My

mother told me I was eighteen months old at the time. My memory shows no more detail than the badly focused snapshots that I used to take with my Donald Duck camera. It seems to me that it is evening, although I can't be sure. My mother is present. I don't remember whether my father is there or not. I am sitting on a chair in front of the fireplace in our home. Dr. Dunno is sitting across from me. He is wrapping my arm.

Mother recounted the trauma leading up to his visit many times. I began walking at nine months. By eighteen months, I had become an unrelenting climber. This I did, my mother said, by pushing a chair over to the countertop in the kitchen, climbing onto it, and then, grasping the handles of the cupboards, scaling hand over hand to those nearest the ceiling.

"Laws, I had to watch you every second," she used to say, reliving her exasperation with my early life.

After noticing this inclination to climb, she carefully kept me away from the area, but on this occasion she turned her back for too long. When she came into the kitchen, I was hanging from a handle on a top cupboard with one hand. She screamed. I let go, fell to the floor, and injured my arm.

In the absence of 911, she called Dr. Dunno, who made an immediate house call. He wrapped my arm, and then informed my parents that such a fall at this early age could result in my arm shriveling into a withered flipper. This possibility worried my parents for many months, and the question was resolved only when it became clear to all that my arm was still growing.

It was not kindly Dr. Dunno's first mistaken call, nor his last. A year later he told my parents that Grandma Swindle, who had had a heart attack, would not live longer than six months. She died twenty years later.

Those relatively benign misjudgments, simply pronouncing an early death sentence that would be commuted by the patient, were not so serious as later mistakes. My father had been short of breath for as long as I could remember. I don't recall a time when he bolted into a sprint or even a short jog. On fishing trips, he would stop several times walking up even a gentle slope to catch his breath. He insisted it was nothing and refused to go to a doctor.

By 1963 his breathlessness had become incessant. He was constantly tired. He visited Dr. Dunno, who recommended a three-day hospital stay for extensive testing. Apparently I had some influence on his decision to have a thorough examination, because I recently came upon a letter my father wrote to me in June after the hospital checkup, berating me for making such a fuss and upsetting my mother. "I am the picture of good health," he wrote, "and you, silly boy, have nothing to worry about. The only thing Dr. Dunno found anywhere was a little spot on my left lung that he says can be cleared up with antibiotics, which he has prescribed."

This "na-na na-na-na" tone dissipated two months later, when Dad vomited blood. This time he bypassed Dr. Dunno and went straight to a specialist. The doctor took the X-rays that Dr. Dunno provided, put them on his screen, and in a nanosecond said, "We've got trouble." The left lung, contrary to Dr. Dunno's diagnosis of a small, curable infection, had a large mass in it.

When my mother returned home after five exhausting hours of waiting for doctors to complete the surgery, she said he had cancer. "They took his whole left lung," she said. "The doctor said he thought they got it all, but if he missed one cell, he wouldn't give him more than a year to live." Dad died fourteen months later.

Inexplicably, for several years afterward I presumed to trust what doctors told me. This is not to my credit. I needed only to have looked back at the numerous experiments I was subjected to for hay-fever cures. My parents had a large lawn, a larger garden, and an abundance of weeds; the place was Pollenville, USA. My chores were to mow the lawn and to help Mother in the garden, clearing weeds and tilling.

When my hay fever became incessant, my parents

took me to Dr. Dunno. He suggested removing my tonsils, speculating that they were the cause of the problem. Other doctors, however, counseled that removing my tonsils might make the allergies permanent. My parents tossed around the idea of a tonsillectomy for a long time and finally decided there was no clear relationship between my tonsils and my allergies.

Still, the hay fever continued and appeared to worsen. My mother turned to a woman in the neighborhood for help. Her name was Rose. Rose, as everyone knew, had had cancer years before. Had her doctors given her up for dead or suggested drastic surgeries that offered little hope? I don't know. In any case, Rose quit seeing her doctors and "cured" herself with herbs and a vegetarian diet that would put her somewhere to the right of Euell Gibbons. Since her miraculous healing, she had become a proponent of herbal cures for all problems.

Sitting with my mother that summer day in Rose's living room, sniffling and sneezing, I felt uneasy. Her restricted diet had given her a skeletal look that became all the more eerie when she smiled. Her teeth stood out from her tightly drawn lips, in contrast to her eyes, which were set too deeply. Still, she was a kind and gentle lady, she spoke softly and with understanding, and I soon felt reassured that I was in good hands.

The solution to my hay fever, Rose said, was

dandelion tea and an herbal powder to be mixed with orange juice and taken daily. She brought out a large can of it for my mother to see.

As they spoke, I imagined myself drinking dandelion tea. Drinking tea was an adult thing to do. It was how sophisticated people in Great Britain spent part of their day. I had seen the pictures in *National Geographic* or *Life*. Hay fever, I supposed in that moment, was not the blight I had thought it to be. It was going to take me into the adult world at age ten. It was a wonderful, magical thing that was happening. I would be the envy of the neighborhood.

As we left I asked my mother how soon I could have some dandelion tea.

"We'll go home and make it right now," she said.

True to her word, she went directly out to the lawn, plucked several big, leafy dandelions, and boiled them up according to Rose's instructions. How long would it take, I asked. Just a few minutes, she said. I stood watching the tea leaves steeping and checking the clock at thirty-second intervals. When Mother finally poured the brew into a cup, it looked wonderful. Could I have it with a little sugar and cream? Of course.

When I took my first sip, I knew my fantasies had misled me. The tea tasted like I now imagine juice from boiled spinach leaves would taste. I gagged, threw the remainder in the sink, and refused to touch the herbal powder my mother had purchased at no small expense. Better to die of a runny nose.

My dad then contacted Dr. Ganzklar, who offered a solution. He had a two-stage cure, which was undertaken at weekly office visits. The first part was to hold pads, about the size of a waffle and connected to a transformer, against my cheeks. Dr. Ganzklar's nurse would then turn up the juice until I said it was becoming painful. She would adjust the power and set a timer for three or four minutes. Not surprisingly, this cleared my head right out. She then gave me a shot and I went back to the garden to mow lawns, hoe weeds, and till, only to become congested again.

Continuing the search for a cure, Dad took me to a local doctor who was treating ailments like mine with radium. It was thought by many to be a miracle cure, a new step in medicine made possible by the advent of the nuclear age. I sat in the waiting room of Dr. Dummwits along with other children, who were playing games with his ample supply of building blocks or reading from his Golden Book collection. Dr. Dummwits explained to my father that enlarged adenoids were the cause of my allergies, and that they needed to be shrunk. This was done by having me put my head back in a dentist-like chair while a four-inch wire with a radium tip was inserted into my nose until it hit against my adenoids. The treatment was performed weekly through the nostrils, ten minutes on each side, as I recall, over several weeks.

This treatment, like its predecessors, accomplished nothing in abating my hay fever, although I learned thirty years later from a doctor friend that patients at a large Chicago hospital who had undergone similar treatments had all gotten thyroid cancer. Another doctor has since confirmed in an examination of my adenoids that the scars from the radiation are still there. Could I still get cancer from this? I asked him. Yes, it was possible that a secondary cancer could appear sometime.

I was then delivered to Dr. Urry. Dr. Urry had come up with a treatment for hay fever that a lot of people swore was working. Dr. Urry, a kindly man with a chipped front tooth, batty eyes that remind me now of Peter Sellers in *Dr. Strangelove,* and a waiting room of sneezing patients filled with hope, explained to me that his method was to help the body cure itself. I was to urinate for one week into a gallon jug and then bring the jug to his office.

I suppose it is an indication of my naive tractability that I went along with this scheme. Other guys, guys like Mr. Touchdown in my high school, I now realize, would have split the scene. "You want what? No way. No way." One week later I appeared in the doctor's office with a jug of urine in a brown paper bag.

The receptionist, who knew all without asking, said, "Name?"

"Tom Plummer."

She wrote "Tom Plummer" unceremoniously on the bag and set an appointment for me in two weeks.

I appeared at the scheduled time. A smiling nurse came into the examining room with a little white box containing half a dozen vials, each labeled with my name and a number suggesting a ratio: 1/500, 1/250, 1/100. She explained that the dosages for my treatment had been calibrated to my body, and that the fluids in the bottles were indeed my urine converted into a formula.

"Have you ever given yourself shots?" she asked.

"No."

"Well, we're going to learn right now." Her voice was chipper, as if "we" were going for a ride on a roller coaster together. She unwrapped a sterile syringe and filled it with the fluid that was about to pass through me for the second time.

"Now," she said, "take this alcohol swab and clean off a spot on your leg above the knee."

This I did, realizing I was now on the roller coaster all by myself.

"Good. That's very good. Now just pretend you are throwing a dart and quickly push the needle into the clean area. If you do it slowly, it will hurt more."

I just couldn't do it quickly. I put the needle against my skin and pressed as hard as I could stand. Nothing happened.

"You have to put more energy into it than that," she said sweetly.

I pushed harder, and the needle went in.

"Very good. Now push down slowly on the plunger until it won't go any further," she said. She seemed almost to be singing her way through this teaching moment.

I pushed down.

"Lovely. Now pull the needle out quickly."

I pulled it out. A little gush of blood followed, which I cleaned off with an alcohol pad and covered with a bandage.

Then, taking out a sheet of paper, she showed me my schedule for the next quadzillion months. "Each day you increase the dosage just as it shows here," she said. "You must sterilize the needle after each use by boiling it. When the needle gets dull, use a new one."

I didn't ask how I would know the needle was dull, but when I bent the first one in my leg a week later, I understood. My Aunt Ruth, a former nurse, gave me some stronger needles she had left over from her working days in the hospital, needles the size of meat thermometers. I used them, squirming and wincing as I jammed them in. After six months of daily treatments,

I took the rest of the formula, which was only about half used, along with all the needles, and threw them in the garbage. Nothing and no one could make me do it any longer.

Eventually my hay fever subsided, which caused me to believe for a while that the whole thing might have been psychosomatic. On further reflection, I realized it went away when I left home and was no longer working in the garden. I have since wondered from time to time why the cure for my hay fever was such a mystery to the adults in my life.

"Well, that was a long time ago," the uninitiated might say. "Things are better now. Doctors don't do that kind of stuff anymore. The FDA controls substances. Mistakes are harder to make."

Indeed. My father-in-law got a hospital notice after a recent surgery saying that his ovaries had been removed.

It would be easy for me to say that the problem lies entirely with doctors, to go on a rampage about their indifference to patients, their costly misdiagnoses, their blight on the human condition. I could, I know for a fact, collect dozens of doctor stories from friends, even from other doctors, and compile a book of doctor atrocities. I could include commentaries on Dr. Mengele and his Nazi medical experiments. The problems with

modern health care, I could argue, lie directly at the feet
of the doctors.

But that's just not true. I know medicine has made
great strides. I know people with new hearts, new liv-
ers, and new kidneys. I know about magnetic reso-
nance imaging and other diagnostic inventions, and I've
benefited from the miracle of arthroscopic surgery.

In fact, I've sat on the other side of the doctor's
reception desk. At the time I made a career choice, I
considered medicine as an alternative. Even well into
my forties I had not come to terms with the idea that
maybe I should have become a doctor. I could no
longer consider a career change, but I wondered what
the life of a doctor was really like. My good friend Jake
is a neurologist, and when we get together for dinner
once or twice a month, I ask him to tell me doctor stories. Neurologists have stories to tell. They deal with
the brain and the central nervous system, and the diseases they encounter are both grotesque and wondrous.
There is, for instance, Korsikoff syndrome. Patients
with Korsikoff syndrome suffer from brain damage that
compels them to fill in gaps of information. A doctor
may hold up her hands as if holding a string and say to
the patient, "What color is this string?"

The patient answers, "Red," although no string is
there.

So when Jake said he needed someone for two

weeks in the morning to transcribe dictation for his medical records, I jumped at the chance. "You're kidding," he said. "I only pay $6.75 an hour. You're a professor. You're a department chair." At the time I was chairing the department of humanities, classics, and comparative literature at Brigham Young University.

"That doesn't matter," I said. "I want to see what really goes on in your office. I can drive to Salt Lake in the morning, transcribe your dictation, and do my work at BYU in the afternoon." It was summer, and things at the office were slow.

The deal was on. For two weeks I got up at 6:00 A.M., did some university work, and left for Salt Lake by 7:30. After seeing each patient, Jake dictated notes that I transcribed from 9:00 A.M. to noon. He would include in his dictation bits and pieces of insight for me about the cases. I learned the names of diseases I had never heard of: Charcot-Marie-Tooth, Kreuzfeld-Jakob, and Kugelberg-Welander.

I learned something about the ins and outs of medical care. Some few doctors, I found out, will give their patients anything they want just to get them out of the office. Patients sometimes came to Jake drugged out of their minds from prescriptions they had badgered their own physicians into giving them. One or two he had to hospitalize while he freed them from addictions. Some patients, I learned, try to scam doctors into giving them diagnoses that will allow them to get workmen's compensation. One man had fallen and hit his head on a gravestone in the cemetery while chasing a dog. He wanted Jake to verify that he was stupider now than he had been before he fell. One woman walked normally into the office, tried to fake a severe palsy in front of Jake, not knowing he could tell the difference between a real palsy and a fake one, and then walked out normally.

My favorite part of the job was when the receptionist was gone and I got to answer the phone. "Dr. Worthmore's office," I would say in my official voice. There was always a pause.

"Is this Dr. Worthmore?" they would say.

"No, this is Dr. Plummer."

When doctors called and I answered, a strong male voice almost always stammered: "Jake?"

"No," I would say, "this is Tom."

"Well, is Jake there?"

When Jake got on the line, they would ask, "Who was that on the phone?"

Jake would answer, "Oh, that's the chairman of the humanities department at BYU. He's my secretary." They would both laugh and laugh, but the doctor calling in never believed it.

After two weeks of this, Jake got himself a real transcriptionist. My last day of work in his office was a

Friday, and I had to leave early so I could be back for the summer convocation exercises of the College of Humanities at 1:00. As a department chair, I was supposed to shake hands with the graduating majors from my department as they received their diplomas.

Driving from Salt Lake to Provo, I thought about my two weeks in Jake's world, a world of Parkinson's disease, Lou Gehrig's disease, multiple sclerosis, and malignant brain tumors—but also a world of phonies trying to beat insurance companies and workmen's compensation with fake illnesses, and a world where doctors kept meticulous records to defend themselves when the lawsuits came.

The contrast between my place in the university and Jake's gave me pause. The Provo Tabernacle, where the convocation was held that day, was filled with beaming, proud parents, broke but happy, and their graduating children, whooping and yelping like dogs in heat. I had left Jake's place of death and sorrow and returned to my place of life and happiness.

It would not do to blame doctors—who day in and day out work to save lives, seeing people in the direst of circumstances, sometimes making mistakes—and exonerate myself, when I make blunders in my teaching that may keep deserving students out of medical school. I have no idea how much damage I have done over the past thirty years in the classroom.

And it makes no sense to absolve myself of responsibility for my body. It's my body. It's a brutal lesson of aging that it all comes down to me. An acquaintance of mine who had a massive heart attack at age thirty-seven once said, "I realized early on that I had to take charge of my own health care." He lived another thirty years. Like the biblical physician, he had to heal himself.

REFLECTIONS ON CONDUCTING MY VIRTUAL FUNERAL

The last place I want to be turned into a joke is at my funeral. Gentle humor in a funeral is fine. I like that. I'm not talking about humor. I'm talking about being remembered for all time as a horizontal joke. Like Nephi Petersen. All my grandmother remembered about old Brother Nephi Petersen in Monroe, Utah, was his funeral, where a speaker who had no ear for metaphor said, "The shell remains but the nut has gone." She told that story at least five times a year, each time laughing and saying, "People say the darndest things." She never said anything about Brother Petersen himself, who must have had a life before his funeral.

She remembered nothing but that the nut had passed on. The one thing I do know about Brother Petersen is that somebody got the wrong guy to speak at his funeral.

That's why I've never liked the idea that others will be in charge of my last moments above ground. With just a slip of the tongue, a well-meaning someone can reduce my life to a dumb joke. Eleven years of piano lessons, twenty-five years of education, forty years of teaching, forty-five years of fathering, and fifty years of husbanding down the drain. One slip of a computer key, and my obituary reads "P-1-u-m-b-e-r"; two slips and it's "B-u-m-m-e-r."

It's not enough that my name was forever the brunt of jokes, that I spelled it thousands of times for bankers, store clerks, and, yes, plumbers. It's not enough that the dumb jokes began in kindergarten, when I didn't even know I had a name that invited potty humor. At the urinal in the boy's bathroom one day, the kid standing next to me said, "Hey, plumber, will you fix my pipes? Ha. Ha. Ha." Is that how it will all end?

I know many people share my anxiety about funerals, because I've often heard mention in funerals that the deceased outlined their own services. The problem is that it must be nearly a deathbed exercise; otherwise your intended participants may die first. Especially if they're old. And then there's the risk that I might die unexpectedly. Just standing at a garden party with a virgin piña colada in my hand and—

"Our loving, father, grandfather, great-grandfather, uncle, and plumber's friend," the obituary reads, "died suddenly at the home of friends after a courageous battle with a virgin piña colada." It's all well-intentioned, I know, but the tone is wrong, the details are wrong, and the plumber's friend joke is so old it doesn't fly any better than a rusted-out Sopwith Camel.

Of course I could create a long list of speakers and performers in order of preference. Odds are that at least some of the people on the list will outlive me, especially if they are much younger, like one or more of my sons. Yet this too seems risky. My sons can be uncouth. My sons know a whole lot more about me than I care to have divulged. Things like how I lined them up to confess a peccadillo and wouldn't let them go until the innocent guy finally gave up and said he did it.

If Ed is telling this story right, it's just another embarrassing chapter that doesn't belong in my funeral. I remember nothing of it, but he claims that one day I set him and his brother Jonathan down in the dining room in the "yellow house" to scold them. They were maybe eight and nine years old. "We were sitting on the carpet by the door that went into the kitchen," he says with all the confidence of a key witness, "and you were chewing us out because one of us had eaten cereal and left the bowl out so that the sugar and cereal had hardened on the bottom. You wanted to know who had left it there. I knew it wasn't me, but Jon wouldn't talk. So then you launched into a lecture on lying and how important it was to be honest, and I thought we would never get out of there, so finally I decided to take the heat just to get away. When I confessed to what I didn't do, you chewed me out for lying by not confessing sooner and sent me to my room. Later Mom came home with Cracker Jacks for everybody. I came running out, but you told me to get back in my room to finish my punishment. Then I said, 'I didn't do it,' which was true, and you chewed me out for lying a second time and sent me back to my room without the Cracker Jacks."

It's all so unpredictable. The one friend I asked to play Bach's "Come Sweet Death" on the viola at my funeral, because his rendition once made me cry, has already died. Will an officiator invite some ignoramus to sing a medley of country songs instead, songs like "Get Your Tongue Outta My Mouth 'Cause I'm Kissing You Good-Bye," "How Can I Miss You If You Won't Go Away?," or "If My Nose Were Full of Nickels, I'd Blow It All on You"?

Even simple things, like closing the casket, require orchestration. Louise says she wants her casket closed to everyone but the immediate family. "I don't want anyone looking down at me," she says whenever the subject comes up. "Dead people look dead. They don't look like they're asleep."

On the other hand, does family get to say good-bye? I went to a funeral once for the sister of Ethel McGregor. Ethel was in her late eighties, had spent a lot of time with her sister, and felt a huge loss when she died of a heart attack. Ethel vented her grief to me because I was her clergyman at the time.

The funeral was Protestant; the particular denomination escapes my memory. Contrary to the tradition in which I was raised, where the family gathers privately before the funeral, has a prayer together, says last good-byes, and closes the casket, this clergy left the casket open throughout the service. At the end, the mourners, including Ethel and her older brother, were invited to file out of the chapel, after which the casket was closed. As I retrieved my coat on that cold but sunny January day in Minnesota, I could hear Ethel asking loudly, in her unmistakable contralto voice, "Did they close the casket? I didn't get to say good-bye. Did they close the casket? I didn't get to say good-bye." Knowing Ethel's capacity for creating dramatic moments, I was filled with foreboding.

At the cemetery, pallbearers lifted the casket out of the hearse and onto the frame that held it over the open grave. The minister recited the Twenty-Third Psalm and offered a prayer. Certainly the freezing Minnesota wind dictated that the service was over. But at that moment, Ethel threw herself upon the casket, gripping the handles on either side and repeating in her inimitable voice, "I didn't get to say good-bye. I didn't get to say good-bye."

The flustered mortician tried gently to pry her off, to no avail. The minister stood by with a helpless look. Mourners shifted feet, teeth chattering. How would this end?

I knew how it would end. I stepped to the mortician and said, "Is that casket sealed? Can you open it?"

"Oh, sure," he said. "But it won't be a pretty sight. The corpse will show blotches in the bright sunlight."

"Look," I said. "I'm this woman's clergyman. I know her. She won't get off the casket until she can say good-bye to her sister. If you want to go home tonight, please open the casket and let her say good-bye."

He stepped to Ethel, who was still draped over the casket, and said, "Ma'am, we'll open the casket so you can say good-bye."

With that assurance, Ethel stepped back. The mortician opened the casket, and Ethel lifted her pallid sister, stiff as a fallen tree, from her bed. "Good-bye, dear," she said, kissed her on the lips, and laid her back down. I didn't remember anymore how cold it was. The rattled mortician closed the casket, and it was finished.

As I walked past Ethel's brother, who had a long-standing hate-war with her, I heard him ask his wife, "Did she just kiss that damn thing?"

So I'm taking control of my funeral. When the time approaches, I'll have a holographic projection made of me conducting the service. The advantage of a holographic projection over a videotape is that it's three-dimensional, virtual reality. It'll look just like me standing up there. The projector will begin running before the funeral begins. I will be standing at the podium quietly, dignified, as clergy are wont to do, looking around as the congregation comes in. I'll be dressed in a dark blue suit with a starched white shirt and red paisley tie, selected by Louise. I'll stand with dignity. Occasionally I'll wave my hand or wink to suggest I've seen someone I know, maybe say in a soft, funereal voice, "There are still a few seats at the front of the chapel." I'll arrange for a real organist to be seated behind me playing "Jesu, Joy of Man's Desiring," until I give a one-minute signal by ringing a little bell to wind down the prelude.

Then I'll ask the congregation to arise while the casket is brought in, followed by mourners. The projector will be on pause during this time, but my poised image will remain in front of the congregation.

When the casket is in place, the holographist will start me running again. I'll invite the congregation to be seated, welcome them to my funeral, thank them for coming, thank the organist for the beautiful prelude music, for using the French-horn stop so effectively, and announce the opening prayer.

I will leave written instructions for the person who prays to be brief and as composed as possible, so that we don't run into the problem I witnessed at a funeral recently. The brother of the deceased gave a lengthy invocation. Moved by his sister's death, he spoke softly and shed a few tears. Near me was a ninety-three-year-old, slightly deaf woman who could not hear his humbly intoned words. Thinking, perhaps, that he was not speaking at all, she said in a loud voice that startled me out of my reverie, "He's in trouble." A moment or two passed, the grieving brother continued to struggle through his sentiments, and the woman prodded him: "C'mon, Harold. Get on with it."

After the prayer I will announce the tribute and two talks—maximum two talks. These are not to exceed ten minutes. I will leave written instructions for speakers that ten minutes means five typed, double-spaced pages. Normal speaking speed is 125 words per minute. A typed page, double spaced, is 250 words. Therefore, ten minutes is five double-spaced typed pages. They are not to "wing it," I will instruct. Write out the talk and stick with the text.

After the talks have been delivered, I will comment briefly on each. "Thank you, Al, for those lovely thoughts. A bit overstated, I think, but really well intended."

"Thank you, Ed, dear son, for your remarks, and thank you for not mentioning yet again that I punished you by taking away your Cracker Jacks."

And there will be congregational singing, con-ducted, I hope, by someone like Betty Homolya. Betty had a heartbeat. Betty was a nightclub singer. Betty sang sexy French songs. When I was young, she conducted the congregational singing in our church on Sundays. She was an abundant woman with long, rococo curls that framed her Rubenesque, beaming face. Unlike the more reserved sisters of the congregation, Betty wore lots of makeup—I remember especially her rosebud lips—an elegant black dress, which revealed just a touch of cleavage, and a brightly colored scarf. When she led the music, her bountiful torso swung gustily to the rhythm, which appealed to my adolescent heart, and she smiled with such radiance that everyone, including teenagers, wanted to shout out those hymns. "Welcome, Welcome, Sabbath Morning." Alas, Betty too has passed away.

At the end of the service, I will thank all for

attending, announce my burial at the Salt Lake City Cemetery, and mention that Louise and I have a single grave plot and that she, according to her lifelong wishes, will indeed be on the top bunk.

My family has emphatically assured me that under no circumstances will they carry out my plan. "It's just weird," they say, almost in unison. "You are so weird. You're out of your mind."

They need time to adjust to the idea. Frankly, I think it could catch on. Like the drive-through mortuaries that started in Las Vegas a few years ago. You drove up to a viewing window, told the mortician whom you wanted to see, and he wheeled the casket over so you could pay your last respects from the comfort of your own air-conditioned car.

I believe my idea offers a solution to an old problem, which I call the paradox of the nut and the shell. I doubt anyone will fall asleep at funerals anymore. Just to be sure, I will insert a line or two into my remarks to keep people on the edge of their seats: "I notice that the gentleman on the tenth row—yes, you—seems to be dozing off. I hope I'm not boring you."

PART 4

CONCILIATION

*"Now is the time for me to rest and play.
I've worked all my days. Now I want to play
these other days out. And God will let me,
too. I'm going to play in my playhouse.
I love it."*

—NELLIE MAE ROWE, IN HER EIGHTIES

Paradise Revealed

The older I get, the more I want paradise. The harder I look for it, the more elusive it becomes. The futile search comes out in the story of a vacation we took in 1999:

We are on the big island of Hawaii, staying for two weeks in the condo of friends. "Come and visit us," they said in December. We're going home on January 11, but you can stay as long as you want."

We scrambled frequent flyer miles together, arranged to be in Hawaii on January 9 to spend a couple of days with them, see them off, and stay until January 25.

Every morning people get up here and say, "Another beautiful day in paradise." The temperatures vary between 70 and 80 degrees. The sky is always blue; occasionally a cloud drifts by, which makes the sunsets more spectacular. This side of the island gets nine inches of rainfall a year. Sunny skies, azure waters, day in and day out. "If I could afford to retire and come here to live tomorrow," I say to our host, Lorin, "I'd do it in a heartbeat."

"But then," says Lorin, "how do you make a contribution to the world? This isn't the real world."

I do not want to hear this response. I've grown up thinking I should make a contribution to society, and I sometimes doubt whether my thirty years of teaching have made much difference to my students' lives. "Oh, yeah," I imagine them saying at some cocktail party, "I took German once. Don't remember a thing. Let's see. I took it from a weird guy. What was his name? Palmer, I think. Yeah, Palmer. And have you read Kafka? Really strange." And for that kind of moving and shaking the world, I'm supposed to go back to a four-season climate that is now in the depths of winter with snow piled high and temperatures ranging from 5 to 35 degrees, and teach students something they will forget overnight?

So I make a stab at answering Lorin. "What do you mean it's not the real world? It's real land, real air, real time. I'll write books. I'll tell stories that make people laugh a little and cry a little. What's more important than that?" Even as I speak it occurs to me that this resort community is a man-made oasis. The real world is all around it. Lava everywhere. Huge black boulders nestled into brownish desert grasses. Developers began working on this part of Hawaii just a few years ago, creating bliss out of an unfathomably violent volcanic past.

Lorin smiles at me like I've got spinach in my teeth, a kind but slightly repulsed smile. I'm now feeling defensive. "What do you do that's so important, Lorin? Why don't you retire and live here? It's paradise."

"We think about it," his wife, Judy, says, entering the discussion. "But we think about family and school for the kids, about where they would find new friends in a resort community. We're not sure it would be a good thing for them."

"Do home school," I suggest. "You'd give them a wonderful education." Judy's kind but stern look tells me this is not an option.

The conversation goes nowhere. Lorin is thinking about his responsibility to society, Judy about her responsibility to the children, and I about my responsibility to my mortal bliss—as long as I can make it last.

Lorin and Judy left for home last night, after watching one last Hawaiian sunset with us, and Louise and I are now alone in paradise, a well-worn Adam and Eve.

Now the conversation will not go out of my head. What's wrong with paradise? What's there not to embrace here for the rest of my life? The place is filled with retired couples, couples who gather for chats about real estate and the stock market and gulp down Chinese chicken salad and pineapple-coconut smoothies at the open-air club café. They bask on beach chairs on the white sand and snorkel to watch cadmium, cerulean, and lavender tropical fish swimming around the coral just a few feet off shore. They cheer when a whale clears the water three hundred yards away and hits the waves with a crash that sends spray a hundred feet into the air. Why not live out your days where seasons of the year and times of the day have as much relevance as an atheist at a tent revival? Louise keeps asking me what month it is. I can't remember, because the weather is always the same from January through December. What does it matter?

Even decisions reach a new level of affability. "What shall we do first today?" I ask Louise as we are slowly waking up. "Should we exercise first, go to the beach first, or write first?" We have decided to write every day so as to keep some semblance of discipline in our lives, some nod to responsibility, although we are falling far short of writing much of anything. "I think," I say, answering my own question, "that we should go to the beach first, so that if I die today, I will at least have been to the beach."

And so by 11:00 A.M., after a relaxed time for dressing and eating toasted bagels with a little ham and provolone, we are sitting on the glistening sand in the white beach chairs with white towels provided by the beach club and a large supply of sunscreen.

But the blissful illusion of the day has already begun to disintegrate. Before leaving the condo I went to a shop to buy clip-on sunglasses. A young guy who looked slightly like a beach bum helped me. "Are you from here?" I asked.

"No, I'm from Oregon. I moved here four years ago."

"How's it been for you?"

"Oh, it's great. Paradise every day. For the first two years I didn't do anything but surf and hang out on the beaches. Then I noticed that not everybody had a tan. Some people spend their time indoors working. So I got a job."

"Too much paradise, huh?"

"Yeah," he said. "You can only take it so long."

Back at the condo, I can't find the electronic gate opener for this secure resort community. Lorin was very specific about where it would be, showed me, and now it's not there. I've picked it up and put it down again absentmindedly. Then I can't find the car key. I'm feeling a little frantic.

"Do you need me to take responsibility for some of the important items?" Louise asks. "You seem to be losing everything."

I don't like being confronted with my periodic instability. "Just give me some space," I say. "I'm okay." My tone comes out harsher than I intended. Louise backs off.

Once in the car, Louise cuts to the chase. "You're driving me nuts," she says.

"Huh?" I say. "What am I doing?" I am vaguely aware of being out of my tree.

"You're acting hyper and goofy," she says. "Why don't you just be sad? I can put up with that."

I am totally unprepared for this assessment. I'm sad? In Paradise? A cartoon by Gary Larson comes to mind. It shows two males on an island. One is a genie-type, an imposing figure with a turban, earring, black beard, and mustache. He has a jeweled belt and a large sword with a jeweled handle and scabbard. His trousers are bloused into black boots. The other figure is a much smaller man whose unkempt hair and beard, tattered shirt and pants, and bare feet suggest he has been stranded on the island for some time. The genie is holding an Aladdin-style oil lamp.

The island dweller is thinking aloud: "Well, let's see—so far I've got rhythm, I've got music . . . actually, who could ask for anything more?"

"What makes you think I'm sad?" I ask.

Her response is quick and sure. "When you are sad, you start acting like an idiot. You lose things. You get careless. Why don't you just be sad?" She gently rubs the back of my head.

I feel a swell in my throat. Yes. I'm sad. Last night Lorin let us read his notes recounting the horrific automobile accident that took the lives of his oldest son, Scott, and Scott's wife, Joanna, and left their two children, Hannah, age three, and Samuel, age one, orphaned. Lorin and Judy, now in their fifties, are raising the children with such dignity and calm that I have been holding back tears ever since we arrived. I'm still sad. I'm sad in paradise, as surely they must be for some part of every day.

With Louise's observation and my renewed awareness of underlying emotions, I am struck with the paradox. I want to believe that paradise is without its troubles, that here is a conflict-free society, a society without the madness of the world beyond it. A society where people have perfect bodies without orifices or even cells, just like you see in magazines, where time and money have no relevance.

It's an old story. We get paradise and we just can't stand it. Adam and Eve had it all. The Garden of Eden in the presence of God. Total joy. Total peace. Lions and lambs lying around together. A seamless world. And then they took the forbidden fruit of the tree of knowledge of good and evil, the very fruit God told them to stay away from, the very thing that insured their expulsion. And they bit into it. Why? Well, of course, Satan tempted them. But why were they even suscepti- ble to temptation? They had it all. Why would they put everything on the line like that?

Maybe because everything has its opposite. Every archetype has a light and shadow side, and paradise, it seems, is no exception. The dark side can addle your brains. Goethe, in his masterwork *Faust,* raises tough questions about paradise. At the beginning of the play, Faust is restless to the point of being suicidal. It is Easter Sunday morning, and he feels nothing but the pain of his ignorance. In his opening monologue, he says he has studied philosophy, jurisprudence, medi- cine, and, "unfortunately," theology. For years he has been dragging his students around by the nose and has learned, in the end, "that we can know nothing." And just as he puts a cup of poison to his lips to end his despair, he hears the sounds of a choir emanating from the church. He puts the cup down and eventually forms a bond with Mephistopheles, a devil-type, who prom- ises to show him the inner workings of the world and give him knowledge just like that offered by the tree in Eden. In exchange, Faust promises that if he should ever stop striving, ever be so content that he wants only to sit and smell the daisies, if he should ever say, "Just linger here, it is so beautiful," then Mephistopheles may drag him off to hell.

Escaping to paradise, lingering in paradise, clinging to paradise is the road to hell. It is the ultimate curse. It's a curse that I don't want to hear about, because a piece of me wants to retire to paradise, to be like the next-door neighbor in Hawaii whose most strenuous undertaking of the day is to practice chip shots on the lawn.

Paradise ultimately dries the bones, rots the brain, and petrifies the heart. Paradise is to be visited and left. Lorin had it right. It is not home. It is a port of call from which one derives new energy, new creativity, and new thoughts to bring home.

I'm Back a Chil'

Recently I took my two-year-old grandson, Harrison Xavier, for a walk around the neighborhood. Harrison is the kind of kid you want to take for a walk. He has big rosebud lips that pucker into full blooms when he says "o's" and "u's," a chunky little body that he presses into you when you hug him, a cherubic face, and a smile that makes his eyes twinkle. He's the kind of kid you want to take for a walk because the neighbors all say "Ooh" and "Aah," and "Oh, how darling," and "Is he *really* your grandson?" And I can hear them thinking, "Tom has such a cute grandson. Tom is a charming guy." Harrison is the kind of kid whose charm rubs off even on his grandpa.

And in taking Harrison for a walk, I had another motive. For just a few minutes, I wanted to see the world as I had forgotten it. I remembered vaguely how I had once seen it. Not the world of horses and buggies or reading by the flickering light of the fire in my log cabin, as my kids might like to think, but a world of sizes. I thought of Princess Alice, the enormous elephant at Hogle Zoo that seemed larger than my parents' house, and her baby, Prince Utah, that died shortly after birth and was stuffed and kept on display. Even that baby elephant seemed a hundred times as tall and a thousand times heavier than I was. I could stand for hours in front of Princess Alice, looking up at her enormous bulk swaying back and forth and fantasizing what would happen if she got loose and rampaged through the building while I was there. Could I find a place small enough to get away from her? Would she tear down the building if she got mad enough?

Ants, by contrast, were the small side of my life. If I felt helpless and vulnerable in front of Princess Alice, I felt omnipotent with ants. I could sit on the sidewalk behind the house and squash them for hours on end. Or I could drop them in a little oil and see how long they survived. I was as powerful with ants as I was helpless with Princess Alice, as vicious as I was timid. I was bigger than big and smaller than small.

Years later I went to the zoo with my nephews. Princess Alice was no longer so big; in fact, she was shorter than I was. How could the wonder of fifteen years before have faded, the proportions shifted so dramatically?

I needed Harrison to recapture a sense of that small world, to visit it if only for a little while. Harrison still knows how to be there without trying, without even thinking about it. He's just there.

On the way out the front door he took my hand, walked to the porch steps, and jumped, whooping and holding my hand tightly. As we walked along, he talked to himself in a kind of chant, clapped his hands, and looked back where we'd been as well as ahead. After a few yards he hollered, "Granma"—he calls both Louise and me "Granma"—"I wanna hold you," which means, "I want you to carry me."

Knowing I couldn't last if I started carrying him—he's just too heavy—I encouraged him to keep walking. Suddenly he stopped, stared at a little rock on the sidewalk, and picked up a small stick, conspicuous for no reason I could imagine. I waited while he examined them.

Soon he was moving again, and suddenly he screamed, "Granma, a bee." He was looking at a box-elder bug on the sidewalk. He lifted his leg, stomped on the bug, and yelled, "Got you!" He looked at me with a triumphant grin.

In a few feet he came upon a dandelion, lifted his foot, and smashed it. He picked another dandelion, examined it, and then pulled it apart. Engrossed in the dissection, he couldn't hear me when I called for him to move along.

At the next house was a broken fence. "Wha' happen', Granma?" he yelled with enough alarm in his voice that one might think he had come upon a corpse.

I turned to walk on, only to hear, "Aaaaa, that's a bug." He stomped on yet another box-elder bug and moved to get another one, making high-pitched yodel sounds.

Then again, "I want you, Granma." I picked him up; he held tightly to my neck and sneezed. "S'cuse me, Granma," he said. "I wanna get down."

He stopped to look at the letters "3rd Avenue" imprinted in the cement at the corner of 3rd Avenue and "J" Street and made a pass at saying what they were—Q, B, C. Then he jumped off the curb as if he were parachuting.

The walk continued with box-elder bugs and other insects crossing his path at their peril. He stopped for a moment to watch a guy mowing his lawn, but he was much more fascinated with the little creatures on the ground all around him. Then he yelled again, "I wanna hold you, Granma." I put him on my shoulders, then on my back, and finally on the ground again.

We were almost home now. We had gone around two blocks in forty-five minutes. As we approached the house, he yelled, "Gimme five, Granma," and held out his hand for me to slap.

As I thought about our walk, I realized that, in addition to his fresh language, spontaneity, and curiosity, Harrison had taken me on a little mythic journey, the kind Joseph Campbell describes, where the hero departs from home, kills dragons, is saved at times by the gods, and returns home victorious.

Harrison gave me a peek into a symbolic world where I once lived, a world that I lost somewhere along the way as well-meaning adults, claiming that rational was right and that reason must prevail over intuition, poo-pooed my fears that bears lived in our basement. By being so completely in his symbolic world, by living it, Harrison knitted my past, my present, and my future together.

I know a few adults who have balanced the world of children and the world of adults. Of television fame, Fred Rogers of *Mister Rogers' Neighborhood* and Jim Henson, creator of the Muppets, come to mind, as do the books and illustrations of Maurice Sendak. Recently I discovered Nellie Mae Rowe, a semiliterate woman who began painting in her sixties and whose art was on exhibit while I was in New York. Her works are filled with brilliant colors, figures of people surrounded by unrecognizable plants and animals, displaced in time and space. The labels next to her works list the artistic mediums: crayon, ballpoint pen, pencil, anything she seemed to have in her hand at the time. Behind Nellie Mae Rowe's works is an artist comfortable with herself, decidedly primal and happy in a world of the unconscious, the dream. "At Night Things Come to Me," she labeled one painting. In a videotape made when she was in her eighties, she says, "Now is the time for me to rest and play. I've worked all my days. Now I want to play these other days out. And God will let me, too. I'm going to play in my playhouse. I love it. . . . I'm back a chil'."

ABOVE THE
CANOPY OF STARS

My ninety-four-year-old Aunt Ruth said to Louise and me recently, "You know, in six years I'll be a hundred."

It came as no surprise to me that Aunt Ruth would say this. Aunt Ruth's frame—all five feet and ninety pounds of it, stands straight up. There's no limp in her gait, no palsy in her hands, no slur in her speech. When I think of Aunt Ruth I think of nursing, because she spent the early years of her life as a nurse, and she remained the family Florence Nightingale. When someone in the house was sick, she came with needles, salves, medications, a whole lot of no-nonsense energy for back rubs, and a conviction that "you're gonna lick this thing." She was at the hospital after Dad's lung surgery to give him massages several times a week.

I watched and secretly wished she would give me one of those vigorous, deep-to-the-core, flat-handed massages that made you know you were alive.

When I think of Aunt Ruth, I also think of raspberries. As a boy, I picked raspberries alongside her in our backyard. My parents had a huge patch that supplied several cases of berries for the family and anyone else who cared to take on the tiny thorns that covered the stalks and made you cautious about where you grabbed hold. I never timed myself, but I suspect I took the better part of an hour to fill a cup of berries. Not Aunt Ruth. She seemed to have magnetic fingers. She would lift the leaves over the berries deftly with her left hand, defying thorns and scratches, and with her thumb and first two fingers of her right hand moving like a fine little machine, pluck every berry without damaging one of them. She attached an old Crisco can to her belt, and I watched with amazement as she filled the whole can while I was still on my first half-cup.

My mother bore early witness to Ruth's speed and endurability in her autobiography. She writes about thinning beets:

My father was a very kind man, but one thing he really believed was that children should learn to work and not be lazy. He was the cashier of the Monroe State Bank, so he had my Uncle Harmon plant his twenty-acre farm in sugar beets. Uncle Harmon asked if Ruth and I would like a job thinning beets. We carried our lunch in a little pail, wore big hats, dresses (in those days girls did not wear jeans), long, black stockings, and button shoes. Mother had made some pads to tie around our knees so they would not get too sore.

Some men blocked the plants so they were ten inches apart. Our job was to crawl up those forty-rod rows [660 feet]—I could hardly see the end—and pull all the plants out of each bunch but the biggest one. The sun was hot and the ground was hard and hot, but we had to keep going to the end of the row, then crawl back on another. We each did seven rows that day. I have never been so tired. Just after dinner Uncle Harmon came and said we had not done our rows good enough, and we would have to do them over. I could hardly keep the tears back. How could I ever earn enough money to buy a new dress for the Fourth of July? We learned to do better, but I always hated thinning, weeding, blocking, and topping beets. I never learned to do them very fast, but my sister Ruth and our friend Leta could work faster than any of the boys or girls. All the farmers wanted to hire them to thin their beets. La Preal, Leta's sister, and I used to beg them to make a little skip on our row. Sometimes they did. That is why, if I help some-one, I say, "I'll give you a little skip." It is a carryover from my beet-thinning days.

So this was Aunt Ruth, the one who gave my mother "skips" in the beet fields, standing in front of me and Louise saying, "You know, in six years I'll be a hundred."

She proceeded to tell us that she'd been up fixing a leak on the roof a few days earlier when her seventy-year-old son came by. They had had a heated argument about her escapades to the roof. "Don't you dare get up there," he told her. "You'll get hurt."

"I told him to mind his own business," she said. "He's the one who's had his knees replaced and can't get on roofs."

"Aunt Ruth," I said to her. "I know how you'll die. You'll fall off the roof when you're 105 and land on your head."

"No," she said, looking me straight in the eye, "I'm going to die with a fishing pole in my hand." She was not kidding. She was heading for Flaming Gorge the next day to fish with her neighbor, as she does several times a summer. "You know," she said, as we were preparing to leave, "We used to say down home, never kick a horse turd, even if it's dry. It might be your uncle."

I don't know what it means, but it says something about feistiness and toughness that characterizes Aunt Ruth.

My mother was her older sister and just as tenacious about staying alive. A couple of years ago I told her about a friend's mother who had died. "How old was she?" she asked.

"Eighty-five," I said.

"Laws," she said, "she shouldn't be dying at that age."

Old age did not keep Mom from working in the large garden that she'd maintained for more than sixty years. She'd don her work clothes, which consisted of polyester slacks that had to be twenty-five years old, an old plaid shirt, some socks that I'd outgrown as a teenager, sneakers that looked like they'd been worn for the assault on Omaha Beach, and a hat. It was not really a hat. It was a straw basket someone had given her that had once contained a pot of flowers.

"I just can't find the right hat for gardening anymore," she'd say. "This is the best thing I've found."

In the last several years of her life, she developed arthritis in her back and hips. Her remedy was to carry a plastic ice-cream bucket along to the garden so that when she knelt down to weed (she never did get very far from thinning beets), she could use it as a prop to stand up again. She'd spend twelve hours a day in that garden in the summer, crawling on her hands and knees, pushing the plastic bucket in front of her so she wouldn't get stranded.

She often talked about the loneliness that set in after my father died. She turned sixty-one the week after his death and was widowed for nearly as long as she had been married. Louise and I moved to Boston to continue schooling, and my sister moved to California. Mother was left in Utah, 900 miles from my sister and 2,500 miles from me. "Do you know how lonely that was?" she'd say over and over after we returned to work in Utah twenty years later. She'd leave a little time for that to sink in before continuing, "I rolled up my sleeves and got right to work. I work like a Trojan. You just can't sit around feeling sorry for yourself."

If I were to put a motto on her life, a metaphor for the way she lived, it would be, "I work like a Trojan."

With role models like Aunt Ruth and Mother, I've been thinking more and more about how I would like to "be" in old age, should I ever attain it.

"Being" may be as simple as sitting in a football game and just enjoying the game, really "being" there, eating a Polish dog with mustard, relish, and onions, "being" with someone you like. Louise and I went to a football game recently. It was a good game because the team we were cheering for won, but that wasn't really the point. We enjoyed just "being" in the fresh air with an emotionally inebriated crowd.

Behind us was a self-employed entrepreneur who throughout the entire game was engaged in conversation with two men sitting near him. They were talking about how to get rich. The discussion ranged from ventures on the Internet to the stock market. Intermittently his cell phone would ring, and I over- heard him say at one point, "Good. Then it's a deal." Yes, he was at the game, could tell his friends he had been at the game, could claim, because he had a ticket stub, to be a football fan, but in reality, he had not "been" at the game. His wife sat next to him, cheering for the home team, but the two of them never exchanged a word.

My heroes are older people who have learned to "be." Florence Pickering is now in her late eighties. I first met Florence in Oregon at a vacation cottage where her daughter Anne and son-in-law Gordon were stay- ing. She was then in her seventies. Florence looked directly at people with her steel blue eyes when she talked. She spoke with a strong, alto voice. She loved walking and stepped out briskly. When she was excited she'd say, "Oh, boy."

Florence had just returned from a tour of church organs in Europe. It was neither her first nor her last. She has stayed in touch with a local university organist she likes, and when he takes people on tours of world organs, she books on. She talked enthusiastically of organ recitals she'd heard on a recent tour to Holland.

"Oh, the organ in den Haag is a wonderful instru- ment. And have you heard the one in Haarlem?"

During this first meeting, Florence saw an end to

her ventures. "I think I'll quit traveling when I'm eighty," she said. "I'll be too old to travel." Not so. She was still going on tour in her mid-eighties and attending university music conferences on organ performance.

I think of a woman well into her seventies who ate in the dining room of the Mayflower Hotel in New York City last Easter. The Mayflower's dining room had elegant carved paneling and lush carpet. Each table had white linen cloths and freshly cut flowers. The woman had her white hair done in a precision cut and wore a fashionable wool suit. She sat at a table next to the restaurant pianist. He was playing songs from American musicals of the twenties, thirties, and forties— Gershwin, Cole Porter, and early Rodgers.

She stayed on after finishing her meal, listening to the piano music, smiling, softly tapping rhythms, and mouthing lyrics. When the pianist finished a number, she would clap, share a few words with him, and listen to the next piece.

I think of a woman I heard about while on the New York subway. Louise and I were going to Gramercy Park. I was checking the map to see where we should get off. An older man dressed in a tailored navy-blue business suit asked if we needed instructions. We got into a conversation. The subject of aging came up, possibly because he was still working as an attorney in his seventies. He said he knew a ninety-eight-year-old baroness who lived in New York City. "As a matter of fact," he said, "she's leaving for a vacation in Rome today. She's traveling by herself."

"How does a ninety-eight-year-old get along in New York City?" I asked. I had noticed that the subways are seldom equipped for the handicapped and that getting around New York could be difficult for an older person.

"Very well," he said. "Of course she has an escort. But she says he's a lousy dancer."

I think of Orrin Tugman, whom I met when he was in his mid-eighties and I was an adolescent. He was one of my father's fishing partners. Earlier he had been known as Dr. Orrin Tugman, Dean of Sciences at the University of Utah. He was a physicist. My father told me to call him Dr. Tugman. I was allowed to go fishing with Dad's group on their summer trips to Pinedale, Wyoming, if one of the foursome couldn't go. Orrin, I think I may now call him that, commanded respect. He stood tall. He had enormous physical stamina. He hiked where everyone else hiked. He ate what everyone else ate. He caught as many fish as anyone in the group.

When my father, at least twenty-five years his junior, lay dying, Orrin came frequently to the hospital to visit. He came just moments after Dad passed away. I met him as he got off the elevator and told him Dad had just died.

"Oh, I'm sorry. I'm very sorry," he said. He shook my hand and stepped back onto the elevator. I thought I would never see him again.

A few weeks later he called Louise and me at our student apartment. He wanted to pay us a visit. A man of distinction, now in his nineties, he wanted to visit newlyweds in their student housing, which had been barracks during World War II. He spent an hour with us. He asked about our studies. He asked about my mother. He thanked us for letting him visit. It was the last time I saw him.

Many years later my mother was still receiving Christmas cards from him. He was living with a daughter in Florida. He was nearly blind, but he could type. He typed his Christmas letters one by one. Mother showed me one. It had a few errors, but it was readable and clear headed. Orrin was 103 when he died.

I think of Uncle Tom, my grandmother's brother. He lived to be ninety-two. Uncle Tom worked hard all his life. He was a caretaker at an amusement park until he was nearly ninety. I had a friend in college who worked side by side with him caring for the gardens there. He said he never worked next to a man, young or old, who worked so hard.

What was remarkable to me about Uncle Tom was not how hard he worked. It was his warmth. Uncle Tom was visiting my family when I came home from junior high school one day. When I walked into the room, he stood up immediately, in spite of his seniority. His face was reddened by the sun; his white hair glistened. He smiled the kindest smile I ever remember seeing, took both my hands in his, and said, "How are you, Tommy?" I felt absolutely loved.

When I meet such people I'm tempted to ask, "How did you get through the despair, anger, doubt, fear, and loneliness of aging?" I don't ask, because I'm sure they would answer that they didn't do it as well as it might appear, that they had rough bumps, swamps, and mountains to negotiate in their lives, and they are still negotiating them.

My mother said sometime in her late eighties, "I've learned the golden years aren't so golden." But I think she, and many like her, have learned that they had to cut their losses and move on. Sometimes she would talk about the hard times, but then she'd say, "You can't just sit around feeling sorry for yourself." These are people who have learned to be buoyant, even cheerful in the face of hard times. What moves them to go on when there is so much to feel bleak about, so many reasons to melt into self-pity? Is it genetic? Is it raw determination?

Surely they have heard the voices of intelligent people crying out that life ends in shipwreck. "Look at the end," they say. "Just look at the end of mankind. There is nothing more. Dust to dust. If there is anything left, it's the chemistry of your body that returns to the earth and reformulates in combinations resembling you not one bit."

I know these indomitable ones have seen the end as well as I have. They have heard the voices of the cynics. I have seen the end in the basement of a church nestled in the greening vineyards along the Mosel River in Germany. The bones of villagers are tossed into a cellar under the church, directly beneath the pews where worshippers sit. You can see them by walking to the side of the church and looking through an iron grate. There they are, the bones of hundreds of people, piled up just as they were discarded.

I have seen the end in picturesque Hallstadt, a minuscule town precariously perched on the steep slopes of mountains that plunge into Halstätter See, a cobalt-blue lake in the Salzkammergut in Austria. Because most of the town clutches to the sharply angled mountains around it, the space for a cemetery is sharply defined and limited.

The townspeople found a solution centuries ago: They dig up the skeletons of the deceased after five years or so and stack them in the *Beinhaus* or bone house next to the church. Before they die, villagers can arrange with the local tole painter, if that's the appropriate word, for a design to be painted on their disinterred skulls, which are stacked separately from the other bones. One skull has a rose painted on it. Another a snake. A third just a name: Schmidt. Former Schmidt. Ex-Schmidt. Tourists may visit the *Beinhaus* for a dollar or so and photograph the remains.

There's no longer anything for the deceased to hide. Their gaping maws display crooked, rotted, and missing teeth, broken and deformed bones, no longer discreetly hidden beneath clothing, and the scars of disease. I was with an orthopedic surgeon the last time I visited the *Beinhaus*. He could read the bones like a book. Their language of scars and blemishes narrated to his educated eye the ailments, pain, and suffering of people long dead. There was no pretense here.

"See how the head of that femur is deformed?" he'd say. "He had Legge-Perthes disease. And there—that bump on the tibia, see that overgrown bone right there? That's Osgood-Schlatter's disease. And there's a lot of osteomyelitis."

"How does that show up?" I asked.

"It's an infection of the bone that causes it to become thick and deformed because the body's trying to grow more bone to heal itself."

Despair seems now to dance around the squirrel cage of my own life, peering in at the most inopportune times, like an unwelcome guest waiting for an invitation to dinner. Writing in her nineties of life in the eighth and ninth decades, psychologist Joan Erikson says: "Despair . . . is a close companion . . . because it is almost impossible to know what emergencies and losses of physical ability are imminent. As independence and control are challenged, self-esteem and confidence weaken" (in Erik H. Erikson, *The Life Cycle Completed,* 1st paperback edition [New York: W. W. Norton, 1997]: 105–6).

Doubt is the root of despair. It feeds despair—doubt in oneself, in one's perceptions of the world, in God. While Prozac and a good psychotherapist may help ease despair, at least for a time, they can do little to assuage the underlying doubt. Doubt has a way of becoming its own reality. It overrides rational, even physical evidence to the contrary and becomes its own self-indulgent demon. "Through doubt," Francis Bacon wrote, "error acquires honor; truth suffers repulse." Doubt becomes prosecutor, judge, and jury, makes a verdict, and exacts a penalty on the most self-evident of truths. Through doubt I fear the future, and so I forget the present. Then I am dead in the present and dead in the future.

I did not see the angry consequences of doubt until my early twenties, when I served a thirty-month mission for my church in Austria. World War II had come to an end only fifteen years before, but it was a war I knew little about. Fifteen years made up about three-quarters of my life. I could scarcely remember anything from fifteen years before. I could barely remember, as a young boy, standing out in the street hitting a pan with a spoon to celebrate the end of the war.

I soon experienced crowds of Austrians who went everywhere on foot. Thousands of others, old and young alike, rode bicycles and mopeds, sometimes with two or even three passengers. Then there were the three-wheeled cars with a door that opened up the whole front end, which people with a little money were driving, and the hordes that daily jammed onto street-cars to get around. These all were just part of the quaintness of Austria to me.

I assumed their routines were normal as well: People bathed once a week with water from a heater that was shut down except on bath days; they squished every bit of toothpaste from the tube by flattening it with a toothbrush; they made toilet paper from newsprint torn into four-inch squares. It was kept in a little box next to the toilet. I learned a lot of German in the bathroom.

Likewise I imagined the hundreds of women I saw every day wearing black armbands, black scarves, black dresses, black stockings, and black shoes to be recent widows who were in mourning. It did not occur to me that many of them were war widows, that they had been mourning for years.

With hindsight I realize that the women of Austria in their black garb were still carrying the emotional weight of the war by continuing to grieve and mourn. They played a different postwar role from that of the surviving men. The men were, in a word, angry. Many of them had served on the Russian front in the darkest hours of the war, when German troops invaded Russia with the intention of capturing Moscow, ravaging and pillaging as they went. The Nazi leadership had drastically underestimated the bitter winter their soldiers would encounter, and they froze by the tens of thousands. One account attributes many of the German casualties to shoes that fit too well. In the cold of winter, the troops could not add enough insulation—stockings or even paper or straw—to keep their feet from freezing. They fell down and died.

The anger of the surviving men, however, was not directed at the Nazi leadership, who had betrayed them in every way imaginable. Their anger was directed at God. "How could God let war happen?" That was the question that they put to us young, naive Americans time and time again. And with the question always came a diatribe against the clergy. "We could see the priests on the enemy side blessing their weapons, while priests were blessing weapons on our side. What kind of God would permit that?"

Their rage baffled me. I had spent the war safe at home in Utah, thousands of miles from the bombs that were raining down daily on their heads. I was incapable of feeling their pain. How could I comprehend the bitterness of the men who had survived the war in France only to be sent to the Russian front?

Over the years a single moment has stuck in my mind that encapsulates all of my encounters with those angry men. One day I met a man with a black patch over his left eye. I had seen hundreds of men with artificial limbs or no limbs, but this was the first time I had talked to someone with an eye patch. He invited my missionary companion and me into his apartment. He emitted a dark tension, an explosive pressure that the ticking timer on a bomb might signal. His dark hair, combed straight back and greased down, and his black, trimmed mustache accented the strain in his tightly drawn face.

He listened to us for a few moments and then held up his hand like a policeman stopping traffic. "There is no God," he said. It was not a statement of belief but a statement of fact. "There is no God. No one but a fool would believe in God."

I asked him why he didn't believe in God. He went into a tirade, gesturing wildly and shouting out the

stories we had heard dozens of times about the con-
flicting interests of priests on the front lines and finally
condemning anyone who could believe in a God who
allowed such things to happen.

Then, almost as if he had rehearsed the scene, he
grabbed hold of his black patch and said, "This is why I
don't believe in God." He ripped it off, exposing a con-
cave socket with only a tiny slit in the skin where an
eye had once been. I sat stunned. "There is no God," he
shouted again. "Nothing."

He was angry at God for not existing.

In a best-case scenario, doubt brings sadness, not
rage, melancholy reinforced by the conviction that life
is by nature tragic and faith childish. Eight years ago I
went to a birthday party for a doctor in Berlin. It was a
garden party in the formal European style, on the gen-
erous patio and lawn of a beautiful villa where
canopies, tables with flowers, and chairs had been set
up around the lighted swimming pool. The guests were
distinguished members of German society, wealthy, well
educated. Among them were corporate executives,
physicians, and diplomats, all self-assured men and
women, the crème de la crème of old Berlin.

I felt self-conscious in this crowd, partly because I
was the only foreigner present and partly because I was
the youngest by at least twenty years. The guests, nev-
ertheless, were forthcoming and warm in asking about

my visit to Berlin, my research, and my background in German culture. Midway through the party I was sitting next to an elegant woman in her seventies who wanted to know how I had come to learn German. I told her that as a young man I had been a missionary in Austria and continued studies afterwards.

"I have a love-hate relationship with religion," she said. She spoke in a quiet, wistful tone.

"Tell me what you love," I said.

She told me that as a child she had lived in Russia, that she and her mother had been devout members of the Russian Orthodox Church. When she was five, the family became refugees and eventually immigrated to Germany. She had recently returned to St. Petersburg and gone to a mass at St. Isaac's Cathedral, the fourth largest single-dome cathedral in the world. She and thousands of others had passed candles from hand to hand in the ceremony. Thousands of candles floating under that great dome. "I felt at one with them," she said. "I liked the feeling. I hadn't felt that way since I was a child." She sat silently for a few moments, her hands tightly clasped.

Then, reversing herself, she said, "I studied religion in philosophy courses at the university. It seems to me it has nothing to offer. What is left for me is arrested in my childhood. I know a few prayers I memorized before I was five. That is all. So now it is something childish to me."

"You should not dismiss your feelings in the cathedral so quickly," I said. "Perhaps they are more than childish sentiments."

"How do you pray?" she asked.

Her question came so suddenly I wasn't sure I had understood. I hesitated.

She repeated the question. "How do you pray? Do you stand?"

"I usually kneel," I said.

"Where?"

"At my bed."

"How often do you pray?"

"Every day," I said.

"And do you speak memorized prayers?"

"No. I just talk to God." I tried to get back to her story. "You really should accept your spiritual feelings from St. Petersburg," I said. "They are not childish."

She shook her head.

For a few minutes we sat together without talking. Looking back, it seems surreal. At the birthday party of an eighty-year-old German doctor whom I had not seen for twenty years, I bonded with a woman over questions of faith and belief. It had come so unexpectedly, so intensely.

Could I claim that my own questions about God

were firmly and finally laid to rest? Or would they re-emerge in times of pain and crisis? Such a crisis came with being forty. I learned from pop-psychology books that midlife brings crisis. The crisis, they said, has many sides: a need for change, new relationships, adolescent children, aging parents, and a sharpened awareness that death is on its way. There is only a limited time to accomplish life's work. All of this brings anxiety, which fuels the crisis of the middle years.

At age forty I was chairing the German department at the University of Minnesota; I was managing a large arts project on "Germany in the Twenties"; I was head of a congregation with six hundred members spread over four hundred square miles; we were in debt; and our children were more troublesome than charming.

I was exhausted and frightened. Life at times seemed ridiculous. I knew that underneath all my exhaustion, anxiety, and hopelessness was a spiritual crisis, but I could not figure out how to deal with it. I had begun getting up at five each morning to read scriptures, looking for answers. I read the gospels over and over—Matthew, Mark, Luke, and John—John, Luke, Mark, and Matthew. I wanted to know what Jesus could tell me. I kept coming back to a passage in Mark 11:22–24, in which Jesus was speaking to his disciples about faith.

"Have faith in God," he said. "For verily I say unto

you, That whosoever shall say unto this mountain, Be thou removed, and be thou cast into the sea; and shall not doubt in his heart, but shall believe that those things which he saith shall come to pass; he shall have whatsoever he saith. Therefore I say unto you, What things soever ye desire, when ye pray, believe that ye receive them, and ye shall have them."

I knew this scripture held the key to my spiritual healing, but I could not figure out why. I copied it and pasted it on the bathroom mirror. I read it while I shaved and brushed my teeth. I recited it while I bathed. I began to feel calmer.

I decided to experiment. I noticed, for example, that Jesus was talking about faith as a dream—a dream of moving a mountain. But why dream of moving a mountain? I continued my recitations. "Whosoever shall say unto this mountain, Be thou removed, and be thou cast into the sea . . ." Then it occurred to me that Jesus was describing the first step in faith: to dream the impossible; to believe in the impossible; to believe that something can actually happen that I know—or think I know—cannot happen. Perhaps dreaming is the first step in faith.

I began to write down my dreams: daydreams, night dreams, half-waking dreams. I wrote a list of wish-dreams I wanted to fulfill:

I want to own an ultralight plane

I want the cabin on Leo Lake on the Gunflint Trail
I want to reduce my taxes to zero
I want to have a pilot's license
I want to write my article by January 1
I want to memorize the Sonatina by January 1
I want to buy a new car
I want to have $20,000 in the bank by June 1
I want to have a supplementary income for summers
I want to be comfortably wealthy
I want to be sexy
I want to have a sabbatical leave
I want to get in better physical shape
I want to have more faith

Some of these, I knew, were self-centered and greedy. I wrote them down anyway.

I continued to think about the scripture and noticed one day that Jesus changed verb tenses while he was speaking. "What things soever ye desire, when ye pray," he said, "believe that ye *receive* them and ye *shall have* them" (emphasis added). "Receive" is in the present tense—right now. "Shall have" is in the future tense—some later time. Why wouldn't Jesus say, "Believe that ye *shall* receive them and ye *shall* have them"? But he was saying something more powerful: "Believe that ye *are receiving* them right now and ye *shall have* them." I looked up the passage in the *New English Bible* and found the difference is even more pointed: "Believe that you *have received* it and it *will be* yours."

It seems Jesus was talking about visualization as a part of faith. As I pray for something, I must believe that I have already received it, and then it will come to me. I thought of a decathlon contestant I had seen in a summer Olympics. Before he did a pole vault he would stand and concentrate. He was trained to imagine himself approaching, jumping, clearing the bar, and landing—and then to do it for real. If he could visualize his jump clearly enough, he could succeed in doing it. Visualization, almost as Jesus articulated it, is now a standard part of sports psychology.

Faith for me had become paradoxical. First I had to believe in the impossible—that I could move a mountain. Then I had to turn this dream into a vision that in my own mind was already accomplished. The idea, the dream, had to become a reality in my mind before it would in fact be fulfilled. If the dream could become a reality in my mind, it could become a reality in my life. The hard part lay in not doubting. "You must not doubt in your heart," Jesus said.

How could I not doubt? I took comfort in another story in the book of Mark, just two chapters before this passage. A man brought his son, who was possessed by a dumb spirit and having seizures, to Jesus to be healed. Jesus said to the father, "If thou canst believe, all things are possible to him that believeth." The father knew his faith was incomplete and said to Jesus, "Lord, I believe; help thou mine unbelief." Jesus then took the son by the hand and "lifted him up; and he arose" (Mark 9:17–27). By grace Jesus had filled in the gap of the father's faith. It was enough to say, "Lord, I believe; help thou mine unbelief."

I went to work on the list of dream-wishes I had recorded. I didn't really want all of them, but within a week I made several of them happen. I didn't reduce my taxes to zero, but I found a good tax lawyer and reduced my tax liability by several thousand dollars. I used that money to take care of other obligations.

I arranged to take a test flight in an ultralight plane—which is just a hang glider with a motor attached. Louise and Sam, my youngest son, came along to watch. My spirit flew with that mosquito-sized machine as I rose over St. Paul, looked out to Wisconsin on the east, to White Bear Lake on the north, and to Minneapolis on the west. It soared because I realized that I had discovered faith would work for me. I had to dream the impossible, think of the future as if it were present, and act.

It was at that moment, with my feet dangling five thousand feet above the ground, that I realized exercising faith meant taking a risk, making a literal "leap of faith."

Is it that very leap of faith, that willingness to take a risk with one's life, the confrontation with the paradox of faith that makes some older people so buoyant? Aunt Ruth climbing on the roof and stating boldly that in six years she'll be a hundred. Mother pushing an ice-cream bucket around the garden so she can stand up when she needs to. A woman who ventures out for a pleasant meal and a little music alone. A baroness who travels alone to Rome when she's ninety-eight. A physicist who accepts young people on their own terms and continues a productive life into his hundreds. The risk is physical, psychological, and spiritual.

The risk is that God may not answer when we knock. C. S. Lewis, writing of his depression at his wife's cancer and death, said he felt at times that knocking at God's door was futile: "But go to Him when your need is desperate, when all other help is vain, and what do you find? A door slammed in your face, and a sound of bolting and double bolting on the inside. After that, silence" (*A Grief Observed* [San Francisco: Harper, 1994], 22).

In those times, when I seem to knock to no avail, I look to the stories of God opening the door that emerge from a community of believers. Sometimes it is enough for me to know that God is still about his work, even if it does not at the moment appear to include me. Sometimes it is good to know that dreams and risks and faith are not the only way of receiving God's help when I need it. Sometimes that help comes unexpectedly, as if by grace.

This was the case for friends who had not anticipated they would need such grace. On August 17, 1983, my colleague James K. Lyon and his wife, Dorothy, were traveling to West Yellowstone in a van with seven of their eight children. About ten miles south of Idaho Falls, their van rolled two and a half times. Jamie, his daughter Elizabeth, and his daughter Rebecca were ejected and knocked unconscious. Within a minute of the accident, a group of vacationers who happened to be nurses and paramedics from the emergency room in an Idaho Falls hospital arrived on the scene. They administered first aid to the family until an ambulance arrived. When Jamie regained consciousness, paramedics had put Elizabeth on life support. He writes: "Dorothy Ann told me that [Elizabeth] was in serious condition and asked me to 'pray mightily' for her."

He continues:

After several hours in the hospital, in which they stitched my head wound and attended to the cuts and abrasions suffered by the children, the doctor treating us invited us to stay in his home outside Idaho Falls—a farmhouse, as it turned out. He was leaving for vacation that same night, so he claimed it was no problem for him. Those of us well enough to be released from the hospital drove to this farm house . . . in a lovely rural setting. Elizabeth had still not regained consciousness and was on life support in the hospital. . . .

On the evening of Sunday, August 21 [three and a half days after the accident], my brother Lynn called from Salt Lake City (we had meanwhile notified the entire family) to tell me of an unusual telephone call he had received the day before. It came from [a man named] Hyrum . . . who had grown up in our [neighborhood] in East Mill Creek and who was friends with my brothers Ted and Lynn. . . . He had great regard for our father, T. Edgar Lyon, and during high school and college he spent many hours in our home and at Dad's office trying to get answers to questions that were troubling him. In some ways Dad almost became a father figure to him. Dad had been dead five years on the morning Hyrum called. Of course Hyrum knew nothing of the accident, but he called Lynn to ask if anything bad had happened to any members of our family. Without answer, Lynn asked him why.

Hyrum reported that the previous night—Friday, August 19 [two days after the accident]—he had a dream in which he saw my father. For reasons he could not explain, he said he saw him in the kitchen of a farmhouse that was not in Utah, but probably in Idaho or Wyoming. He recognized my father easily, but he did not recognize the young woman next to him. My father, he continued, *had his arm around this young woman in a loving, tender way. It made Hyrum think that this young woman, who looked frightened and confused, might have been a granddaughter. . . . He claimed that she appeared to be fourteen or fifteen years old, and that she had auburn hair. That was the extent of the dream, but it was so vivid that he wanted to get in touch with one of the Lyon brothers to find out if something had happened.*

Elizabeth was fourteen years old at this time. . . . She also had auburn hair. [Later] that day, Sunday, August 21, when Lynn called, the doctors informed us that there had been no change in Elizabeth's condition, and that the monitor showed no brain activity. Occasionally there had been some twitches and movement, but we were told that in all likelihood she was no longer alive.

Before allowing the doctors to disconnect the life-support system, Jamie talked with the nurse paramedic who first arrived on the scene. He continues:

They told me that when they first began treating her, her eyes did not respond to light, . . . a sign that there is no brain activity. Gradually we began to realize that she probably died at the scene of the accident . . . probably within minutes of being thrown from the car. . . . The life-support system kept her breathing, and it appeared from the occasional movement that she was still alive.

For the Lyons, this experience was a spiritual confirmation, though not one they had sought. They then allowed medical personnel to disconnect the life-support system, and Elizabeth was declared officially dead on August 22nd. Jamie writes:

Hyrum's dream seems to have confirmed that, since it occurred somewhere between thirty and forty-six hours after the accident. He was surprised and somewhat upset to hear my brother Lynn tell him about it. At the time of his dream, of course, neither we nor Lynn knew she was dead. In fact, we had every reason to believe that she was not. For us, however, the dream confirmed what we later reconstructed about her death, and it seems likely that she was indeed with her grandfather.

This story rings true to me. It rings true because God shows himself to be an observer of human events but not a meddler. He allows tragedy to take its course. He allows war to take its course. These are the natural consequences of being human. To interfere, to prevent tragedy, to prevent war, would be for God to deprive human beings of experiencing fully the life he gave. What could we then possibly learn about the goodness of good and the evilness of evil, about the joyfulness of joy and the sorrow of grief? How could we ever come to feel the great emotional and spiritual depths and heights of life? Without pain and suffering, without hardship, can life be anything but shallow?

A family prays mightily for a daughter's life, yet she dies. God does not bring her back, but he gives the parents the comfort and assurance they need to let their daughter go through a dream that made Hyrum an unwitting mediator. It rings true because it acknowledges both suffering and loss, gratitude and joy, and allows them all to coexist. It allows the paradoxes of life to be.

Some might say that God in this account is unfair. He doesn't do the same for every grieving family. Where are the dreams and visions in behalf of other victims of accidents and violence? Where are their angels? I did not have a visitation from my deceased mother, whom I longed to see just once more. The wife of a friend who died of cancer did not hear any more from him after his death. For most of us, there is no more. Death is the Great Silencer. I don't know why some few receive such messages and others do not. But I would rather know of one good family who had that communication than of none. I am stronger for hearing the story than I would be without it. I feel God's love and God's grace for all people through the Lyons' story. It mediates God's care.

I cling to their story and others like it. I cling to the story of the man who begs Jesus to fill in the gaps of his unbelief. I cling to the words of Job: "I know that my redeemer liveth" (Job 19:25). I cling to these because I know that when I face the last moments of my life, I will be weak. I will need God's grace, in whatever form he cares to impart it, to cope with the degradation of aging and dying. It may not be the grace that comes from a friend's inspired dream in my behalf. It may not be the grace of a divine manifestation. But in their absence, I hope for the grace that comes from loving family and friends, from a community of believers who, in God's behalf, extend a hand when I can no longer help myself, who continue in faith and dedication to God, whom we love but whose ways we cannot comprehend, a loving Father who, in the words of Schiller's "Ode to Joy," "must dwell above the canopy of stars."

A Basket
Full of Posies

All of life leads to memories. The infant has no memories, just energy. The aged person has no energy, just memories. My father drilled into me the importance of memory long before I can remember him doing it. I found in his papers a compilation of poems, aphorisms, and scenes from dramas that he had memorized by the time he was twenty-six. It was nearly two hundred typed pages, dedicated to his mother. He could memorize the names of his students in each class by going through the list once. Even more astonishing to me, he never forgot them. I recall once being in a shoe store with him. The clerk asked if Dad knew his name. He said, "Yes, you are Scotty McIntyre." He had been Dad's student some twenty years before.

I don't have that gift, but it seems I have always

known that I will evolve toward a compilation of memories, and that the breadth and depth of those memories is the treasury of my old age. The loss of memories is akin to dying. An older man whose wife is suffering from Alzheimer's said to me recently, "She doesn't remember the day we got married. She doesn't remember having children. She has no memory. She has no life."

From the onset of our marriage, Louise and I have shared a drive to create memories, often by impromptu gestures that have gotten us in a lot of trouble. When we realize we are in deep water we say, "We really have to be more responsible. Life isn't supposed to be a joyride. We have to plan our lives and stick with the plan." But we never do it. The minute we set up a plan, we undermine it. Fact is, long-term planning feels a lot like killing the possibilities for rich memories. We prefer to take things as they come. Like the lilies of the fields.

This attitude led us to our first crisis. When we moved from historic Boston to midwestern Minneapolis in 1970, we shifted from life as a carefree, childless couple to life as parents of two infant sons, from driving the Maine coast to the beach at Ogunquit and the lighthouse at Bar Harbor to cruising the specials on diapers, Gerber's, and formula in the Red Owl grocery store. Autumn days degenerated from discovering antique shops and roadside stands with maple syrup and fresh apple cider in old Vermont to locating wood preservatives in aisle 3B of the True Value hardware store to keep our rotting house from collapsing in the Minnesota winter. This was not the "happy-ever-after" we had dreamed of. The prospects of life in our new middle-class status with all the accoutrements of normalcy seemed altogether dismal. The anxiety of a predictable life set in: marriage—kids—house—career—grandkids—great-grandkids—die. We had already knocked off four of the seven on the list. How would sterile routines produce memories of any worth?

So when I woke up one Thursday morning in early October 1971 and said to Louise, "Let's drive to Salt Lake for general conference" (a semiannual meeting of our church), she shot out of bed with the might of Wonder Woman, jumping and romping around the bedroom yelling, "We're not dead yet, we're not dead yet."

Within the hour I had gotten a substitute for my Friday classes, and by late afternoon we were headed down I-35 in our yellow VW Super Beetle with its sunroof and automatic stick shift. Louise had christened the car Wanda because of its wan, yellow color.

We bedded the two boys, ages one and two, in the back. The Volkswagen interior had a rear seat with a window well, maybe fifteen inches wide and two feet deep, behind it. We made a bed for Edmund, the baby, in the well and another for Jonathan, the older baby, on the seat. They would sleep through the night, we reasoned, since we had provided all the comforts of a Pullman car. The gentle rocking of Wanda across the great midwestern plains would lull them to sleep as surely as any cradle in a treetop.

We had gotten just beyond the southwest exit of the belt route around the Twin Cities when the kids fouled their diapers. Both at the same time. We pulled to the side of the road, changed them over their protests—kicking and screaming on the hood of the car—laughed at the comedy of our own scene, and drove on.

Contrary to plans, the boys did not settle into the wonderful beds we had made for them. The Great Plains did not lull them. They did not sleep through the night. They bounced up and down, their little heads poking up and around the seats incessantly. We fed them bottles of milk, juice, and cereal, changed their diapers again and again, confident they would eventually fall asleep. They never did. When we arrived in Salt Lake thirty hours later, we were exhausted and nearly delirious.

We sat with our incredulous parents, who were thrilled to see us but afraid we had flipped our lids, and watched televised church meetings for two to three minutes at a time between dozes.

By Sunday afternoon, as we were preparing to leave,

Louise's parents had seen a benefit to our journey. They had planned a trip to Holland to see Louise's paternal grandmother, who was ill, but had found no way of leaving supervision for their youngest two children, Marilyn and David. Could Louise, they wondered, stay on for a couple of weeks with our two sons and take care of her young siblings while they made a quick visit to Utrecht?

So that afternoon I climbed back into Wanda sans wife and sons and headed home. I remember little about the drive. I believe I made a stop in North Platte, Nebraska, the first night and arrived in Minneapolis near midnight the next evening. I was so exhausted that I drove right past the street to our house and became lost for a few minutes trying to figure out where I had gone wrong.

Louise and I kept contact by telephone for the next days. Then one night, at the time I expected a call from her, my mother called. "Tom," she said, "the strangest thing happened today." My mother, as I could tell by her tone, was trying to break some news. "Louise has broken her leg," she said. "She's in surgery at this very moment." She proceeded to tell me that Louise had been at home with our two boys. Her brother and sister were in school. She had just put Ed down for a nap and was carrying Jonathan down the steep stairs in her parents' house when she slipped. In an effort to protect

Jonathan from being hurt, she twisted, fell, and broke her leg in three places, a classic spiral ski fracture, the orthopedic surgeon had said. Sitting at the bottom of the stairs in white-knuckle pain with her leg in pretzel shape, she asked Jonathan, barely two, to bring her the phone.

The phone in her parents' house was around the corner and down a short hallway from where she sat. She had tried to move but the pain from shifting bones was too great. She heard Jonathan walk to the phone, pick it up, and put it down again. "Jonathan, bring me the phone," she said as calmly as she could. "Bring me the telephone." Again he picked up the receiver and put it down. After two more attempts, he got the drift, picked up the phone, which had a long extension cord, and brought it to her. Louise called an ambulance.

My mother recounted the ensuing events many times. She and Louise's sister Janie were at a meeting at the church a block away. "Then," she would say, "these two ambulance men in white coats came in the door and asked if Mrs. Plummer was there. Janie and I jumped up and ran down to the Rooses' house as fast as we could. Janie just ran like a little deer."

Louise, I was to learn over the next several days, would be bedridden for weeks. Healing would take months. The Demerol she took for pain nauseated her, and she felt like she was floating on the ceiling.

Although her parents had returned, she wanted to come home. Four weeks later I flew back to Salt Lake to pick up Louise and the boys. Louise lay pale and fragile on a bed in her parents' house. This was not the woman I had seen the month before, jumping around the bedroom and hollering, "We're not dead yet." Her cast extended in a conical mass of plaster from her toes to her hip. Three bumps in the lower section were "pins" holding the bones together. I now choke in that scene in *An Affair to Remember* when Cary Grant finds Deborah Kerr, after a long separation, crippled in her apartment.

Flight personnel carried Louise on a stretcher onto the plane for the return trip home. Our once joyous adventure entered its healing stages, which would last through the long Minnesota winter of 1972 and into the spring. My mother accompanied us to Minneapolis, and although this was a help temporarily, it could not last. Louise needed to recover on her own, to take charge of her life at home, and we needed to rebuild a relationship that had undergone its first trauma in our seven years of marriage.

Eventually Louise's leg healed. For years, the whole scene was just a memory, fading with the new concerns of middle age. But the orthopedic stress of Louise's fractures returned in the early 1990s as a traumatic arthritis in her right ankle. After four years of increasing pain and incapacity, she underwent surgery to fuse the ankle, which meant screwing its bones together into a fixed position. This prevented her from wearing many of the dress shoes that she liked and launched a constant search for shoes that looked good and felt reasonably comfortable. It has become her cross to bear.

I ask her occasionally as we go for a walk and she deals with the pain of this once perfectly healthy ankle, "If you had it to do over, would you get up on Thursday morning, pack up the kids, and drive to Salt Lake from Minneapolis?" The first answer that occurs to me is always the same: No way. But almost as quickly, other questions pop into my head: Would I really live an absolutely safe life, a life without risk, without adventure? Would I really want to plateau out, live each day like the one before? Where then are the memories?

Louise's answer to the question is more honest. "Of course," she says, "At least we knew we weren't dead yet."

And so, for richer or for poorer, in sickness or in health, we drift toward old age, clutching to a basket of posies that make up the memories of our lives. Once in a while we pluck one out, examine it, reminisce, and put it in a vase on the mantel for old time's sake until we are ready to replace it with another.

I was probably thinking about such posies one

afternoon when Louise and I were strolling through the Naglergasse in Vienna, a narrow little street of beautiful old rococo buildings where outdoor restaurants with multicolored umbrellas give respite to afternoon visitors. We knew without saying the words that we would remember this place. I asked, "If I die first, will you come back to Europe?"

"Oh, yes," she said. "Probably not alone, but I think I'd come back." She paused while we looked in the window of an antique store. "But maybe not. Maybe I'd go back to all the other places where we lived and loved to be together and visit them. I'd go to Minnesota and see all the houses we lived in. Or to Boston and New York and Maine. I'd miss you." We walked along holding hands while a little afternoon rain began to fall.